Student Success Manual to accompany ELEVENTH EDITION

Interplay

The Process of Interpersonal Communication

Ronald B. Adler
Santa Barbara City College

Lawrence B. Rosenfeld
University of North Carolina at Chapel Hill

Russell F. Proctor II
Northern Kentucky University

Prepared by
Leah E. Bryant
DePaul University

New York   Oxford
OXFORD UNIVERSITY PRESS
2010

Oxford University Press, Inc., publishes works that further Oxford University's
objective of excellence in research, scholarship, and education.

Oxford   New York
Auckland   Cape Town   Dar es Salaam   Hong Kong   Karachi
Kuala Lumpur   Madrid   Melbourne   Mexico City   Nairobi
New Delhi   Shanghai   Taipei   Toronto

With offices in
Argentina   Austria   Brazil   Chile   Czech Republic   France   Greece
Guatemala   Hungary   Italy   Japan   Poland   Portugal   Singapore
South Korea   Switzerland   Thailand   Turkey   Ukraine   Vietnam

Copyright © 2010 by Oxford University Press, Inc.

Published by Oxford University Press, Inc.
198 Madison Avenue, New York, New York 10016
http://www.oup.com

Oxford is a registered trademark of Oxford University Press

ISBN 978-0-19-538490-1

Printing number: 9 8 7 6 5 4 3 2 1

Printed in the United States of America
on acid-free paper.

Table of Contents

INTRODUCTION

LEARNING STYLES

People learn in different ways. Some understand best by reading (and re-reading), while others prefer listening to explanations. Still others get the most insight from hands-on experiences. Knowing your preferred way to take in and learn information can contribute to your college success. You might prefer to see information, to hear information, or to work with information in a hands-on way. In college you won't always be able to choose how information comes to you. Professors require lectures, textbooks, essays, labs, videos, and readings. In this section we'll help you understand your preferred learning style and help you discover ways to approach your studies that will work best for you.

In the next few pages we introduce five learning preferences and provide the opportunity for you to identify your own preference. Then you can put that information to work for you. There are many approaches to learning styles and preferences; here we present one of them, VARK, an acronym for Visual, Aural, Read/Write, and Kinesthetic ways of learning. A fifth category, multimodal, recognizes learners who have two or more strong preferences. No approach is better or worse than others; this is an opportunity to identify your learning preference and use that information to facilitate your college success.

The best way to begin is to identify your learning preference. You can do this by completing the following questionnaire.

The VARK Questionnaire

This questionnaire aims to find out something about your preferences for the way you work with information. You will have a preferred learning style, and one part of that learning style is your preference for the intake and output of ideas and information.

Choose the answer that best explains your preference and circle the letter next to it. Please circle more than one if a single answer does not match your perception. Leave blank any question that does not apply, but try to give an answer for at least ten of the thirteen questions

When you have completed the questionnaire, use the marking guide to find your score for each of the categories, Visual, Aural, Read/Write, and Kinesthetic. Then, to calculate your preference, use the scoring chart.

1. You are about to give directions to a person who is standing with you. She is staying in a hotel in town and wants to visit your house later. She has a rental car. You would

   a. draw a map on paper
   b. tell her the directions
   c. write down the directions (without a map)
   d. collect her from the hotel in my car

2. You are not sure if a word should be spelled "dependent" or "dependant." You would

 a. look it up in the dictionary
 b. see the word in my mind and choose by the way it looks
 c. sound it out in my mind
 d. write both versions down on paper and choose one

3. You have just received a copy of your itinerary for a world trip. This is of interest to a friend. You would

 a. phone her immediately and tell her about it
 b. send her a copy of the printed itinerary
 c. show her on a map of the world
 d. share what I plan to do at each place I visit

4. You are going to cook something as a special treat for your family. You would

 a. cook something familiar without the need for instructions
 b. thumb through the cookbook looking for ideas from the pictures
 c. refer to a specific cookbook where there is a good recipe

5. A group of tourists has been assigned to you to find out about wildlife reserves or parks. You would

 a. drive them to a wildlife reserve or park
 b. show them slides and photographs
 c. give them pamphlets or a book on wildlife reserves or parks
 d. give them a talk on wildlife reserves or parks

6. You are about to purchase a new stereo. Other than price, what would most influence your decision?

 a. the salesperson telling you what you want to know
 b. reading the details about it
 c. playing with the controls and listening to it
 d. it looks really smart and fashionable

7. Recall a time in your life when you learned how to do something like playing a new board game. Try to avoid choosing a very physical skill, like riding a bike. You learned best by:

 a. visual clues—pictures, diagrams, charts
 b. written instructions
 c. listening to somebody explaining it
 d. doing it or trying it

8. You have an eye problem. You would prefer the doctor to

 a. tell me what is wrong
 b. show me a diagram of what is wrong
 c. use a model to show me what is wrong

9. You are about to learn to use a new program on a computer. You would

    a. sit down at the keyboard and begin to experiment with the program's features
    b. read the manual which comes with the program
    c. telephone a friend and ask questions about it

10. You are staying in a hotel and have a rental car. You would like to visit friends whose address/location you do not know. You would like them to

    a. draw me a map on paper
    b. tell me the directions
    c. write down the directions (without a map)
    d. collect me from the hotel in their car

11. Apart from the price, what would most influence your decision to buy a particular book?

    a. I have read it before.
    b. A friend talked about it.
    c. I quickly read parts of it.
    d. The way it looks is appealing.

12. A new movie has arrived in town. What would most influence your decision to go (or not go)?

    a. I heard a radio review about it.
    b. I read a review about it.
    c. I saw a preview of it.

13. Do you prefer a lecturer or teacher who likes to use:

    a. a textbook, handouts, readings
    b. flow diagrams, charts, graphs
    c. field trips, labs, practical sessions
    d. discussion, guest speakers

The VARK Questionnaire—Scoring Chart

Use the following scoring chart to find the VARK category that each of your answers corresponds to. Circle the letters that correspond to your answers. For example, if you answered b and c for question 3, circle R and V in the question 3 row.

Question	a category	b category	c category	d category
3	A	R	V	K

Scoring Chart

Question	a category	b category	c category	d category
1	V	(A)	(R)	K
2	(R)	V	(A)	K
3	A	(R)	V	K
4	K	V	(R)	
5	(K)	V	(R·)	A
6	A	(R)	K	V
7	V	(R)	A	K
8	(A)	V	K	
9	K	(R)	A	
10	V	A	(R)	K
11	K	(A)	(R)	V
12	A	(R)	V	
13	(R)	V	K	(A)

Calculating Your Scores

Count the number of each of the VARK letters you have circled to get your score for each VARK category.

Total number of **V**s circled = 0   (Visual score)

Total number of **A**s circled = 5   (Aural score)

Total number of **R**s circled = 12   (Read/write score)

Total number of **K**s circled = 1   (Kinesthetic score)

Calculating Your Preferences

Because you can choose more than one answer for each question, the scoring is complex. It can be likened to a set of four stepping stones across water.

1. Add up your scores: V + A + R + K = 18   (total)

2. Enter your scores from highest to lowest on the stones below, with their V, A, R, and K labels.

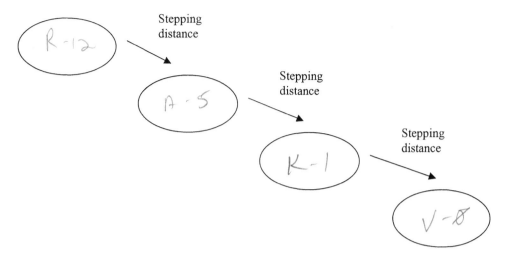

3. Your stepping distance comes from this table.

Total of my four VARK scores is	My stepping distance is
10–16	1
17–22	2
23–26	3
More than 26	4

4. Your first preference is your highest score, so check the first stone as one of your preferences

5. If you can reach the next stone with a step equal to or less than your stepping distance, then check that one too. Once you cannot reach your next stone, you have finished defining your set of preferences.

Now that you've scored your questionnaire, find the help sheet in the following pages that matches your preferred learning style. Go to the help sheet for each preference you have checked. If you have more than one preference checked, you should also read the material on multimodal preferences. Look at the specific strategies to study and learn (intake) information during class and independent study and then become familiar with and practice ways that will help you do well on exams (output). Read more about this resource for learning at www.vark-learn.com.

Visual Study Strategies

You want the whole picture, so you are probably holistic rather than reductionist in your approach. You are often swayed by the look of an object. You are interested in color, layout, and design, and you know where you are in your environment. You are probably going to draw something.

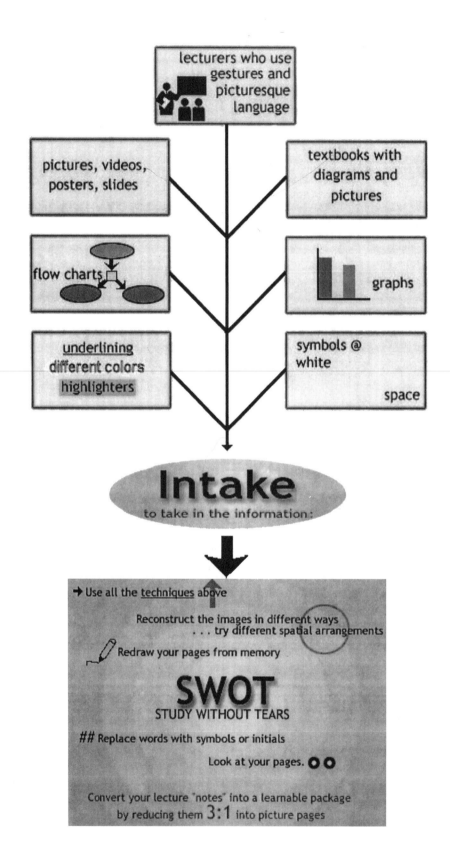

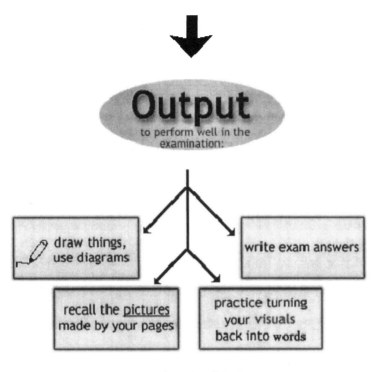

Aural Study Strategies

If you have a strong preference for learning by aural methods (**A** = hearing**)**, you should use some or all of the following:

INTAKE
To take in the information:

- Attend classes
- Attend discussions and tutorials
- Discuss topics with others
- Discuss topics with your teachers
- Explain new ideas to other people
- Use a tape recorder
- Remember the interesting examples, stories, and jokes
- Describe the overheads, pictures and other visuals to somebody who was not there
- Leave spaces in your notes for later recall and "filling"

SWOT—Study Without Tears
To make a learnable package:

Convert your notes into a learnable package by reducing them (3:1).

- Your notes may be poor because you prefer to listen. You will need to expand your notes by talking with others and collecting notes from the textbook.

- Put your summarized notes onto tapes and listen to them.
- Ask others to "hear" your understanding of a topic.
- Read your summarized notes aloud.
- Explain your notes to another "aural" person.

OUTPUT
To perform well in any test, assignment, or examination:

-
- Imagine talking with the examiner.
- Listen to your voices and write them down.
- Spend time in quiet places recalling the ideas.
- Practice writing answers to old exam questions.
- Speak your answers aloud or inside your head.

You prefer to have this entire page explained to you. The written words are not as valuable as those you hear. You will probably go and tell somebody about this.

Read/Write Study Strategies

If you have a strong preference for learning by reading and writing, you should use some or all of the following:

INTAKE
To take in the information:

- lists
- headings
- dictionaries
- glossaries
- definitions
- handouts
- textbooks
- readings—library
- notes (often verbatim)
- teachers who use words well and have lots of information in sentences and notes
- essays
- manuals (computing and laboratory)

SWOT—Study Without Tears
To make a learnable package:

Convert your notes into a learnable package by reducing them (3:1).

- Write out the words again and again.
- Read your notes (silently) again and again.
- Rewrite the ideas and principles into other words.
- Organize any diagrams, graphs, figures, or pictures into statements, for example,. "The trend is . . ."
- Turn reactions, actions, diagrams, charts, and flows into words.
- Imagine your lists arranged in multiple-choice questions and distinguish each from each.

OUTPUT
To perform well in any test, assignment,
or examination:

- Write exam answers.
- Practice with multiple-choice questions.
- Write paragraphs, beginnings, and endings.
- Write your lists (a, b, c, d; 1, 2, 3, 4).
- Arrange your words into hierarchies and points.

You like this page because the emphasis is on words and lists. You believe the meanings are within the words, so any talk is okay, but this handout is better. You are heading for the library.

Kinesthetic Study Strategies

If you have a strong kinesthetic preference for learning, you should use some or all of the following:

INTAKE
To take in the information:

- all your senses—sight, touch, taste, smell, hearing
- laboratories
- field trips
- field tours
- examples of principles
- lecturers who give real-life examples
- applications
- hands-on approaches (computing)
- trial and error
- collections of rock types, plants, shells, grasses . . .
- exhibits, samples, photographs . . .
- recipes—solutions to problems, previous exam papers

SWOT—Study Without Tears
To make a learnable package:

Convert your notes into a learnable package by reducing them (3:1).

- Your lecture notes may be poor because the topics were not "concrete" or "relevant."
- You will remember the "real" things that happened.
- Put plenty of examples into your summary. Use case studies and applications to help with principles and abstract concepts.
- Talk about your notes with another kinesthetic person.
- Use pictures and photographs that illustrate an idea.
- Go back to the laboratory or your lab manual.
- Recall the experiments, field trips, etc.

OUTPUT
To perform well in any test, assignment, or examination:

- Write practice answers and paragraphs.
- Role play the exam situation in your own room.

You want to experience the exam so that you can understand it. The ideas on this page are only valuable if they sound practical, real, and relevant to you. You need to do things to understand.

Multimodal Study Strategies

If you have multiple preferences, you are in the majority, as somewhere between 50 and 70 percent of any population seems to fit into that group.

Multiple preferences are interesting and quite varied. For example, you may have two strong preferences, such as VA or RK, or you may have three strong preferences, such as VAR or ARK. Some people have no particular strong preferences, and their scores are almost even for all four modes. For example one student had scores of $V = 9$, $A = 9$, $R = 9$, and $K = 9$. She said that she adapted to the mode being used or requested. If the teacher or supervisor preferred a written mode, she switched into that mode for her responses and for her learning.

So, multiple preferences give you choices of two, three, or four modes to use for your interaction with others. Some people have admitted that if they want to be annoying, they stay in a mode different from the person with whom they are working. For example, they may ask for written evidence in an argument, knowing that the other person much prefers to refer only to oral information. Positive reactions mean that those with multimodal preferences choose to match or align their mode to the significant others around them.

If you have two dominant or equal preferences, please read the study strategies that apply to your two choices. If you have three or four preferences, read the three or four lists that apply. You will need to read two, three or four lists of strategies. For people with multimodal preferences it is necessary to use more than one strategy for learning and communicating. They feel insecure with only one. Alternatively, those with a single preference often "get it" by using the set of strategies that aligns with their single preference.

There seem to be some differences among those who are multimodal, especially those who have chosen fewer than seventeen options. If you have chosen fewer than seventeen of the options in the questionnaire you may prefer to see your highest score as your main preference—almost like a single preference. You are probably more decisive than those who have chosen seventeen-plus options.

Summary of VARK Scores

Now that you are familiar with your preferred learning style, come back to these pages and review the activities that will help you learn and process information best. Your favorite learning style may not match the teaching style used by the professor in this course. If that's the case, take the initiative to learn the material in the other ways outlined for you in the preceding pages while you continue to develop your ability to learn in ways that aren't your favored method.

Based on what you learned about your preferred learning method, list five specific things you can do to help yourself learn the material in this communication course.

1.

2.

3.

4

5.

STUDY SKILLS

Academic success doesn't just depend on how smart you are or how hard you work: it also depends on how *well* you study. Many students spend hours with their books but don't manage to understand the material they're expected to know. Not all methods of "spending time" with the text are equally productive, so we present here several methods that can help you study effectively.

Use SQ3R

SQ3R is a widely used acronym for an effective method to study a text. The method includes these five steps:

S-Survey
Q-Question
R-Read
R-Recite
R-Review

Survey

Begin by getting an overview of the material you'll later study in detail. Start with one chapter. Look at the title of the chapter and the major headings. Survey the opening page with its Chapter Highlights and objectives. Skim the chapter's tables, photos, cartoons, sidebars, figures, charts, and summaries. Glance at the Critical Thinking Probes and Ethical Challenges. At the end of each chapter, peruse the Key Terms, Activities, and Resources. This big-picture survey will help you put each section of the chapter in a larger context.

Question

Go back over the headings you have just surveyed and turn each one into a question. Most questions will include one of the following words: who, what, when, where, how, or why. Look how headings from *Understanding Human Communication* can fit into these forms:

- Who has power in groups? (Power in Groups, Chapter 9)
- What are the ways to help others when they have problems? (Empathic Listening, Chapter 4)
- When should you reveal personal information, and when should you keep it to yourself? (Guidelines to Appropriate Self-Disclosure, Chapter 6)
- Where can you find information for your speech? (Gathering Information, Chapter 10)
- How can you paraphrase? (Informational Listening, Chapter 4)
- Why is misunderstanding so common? (The Language of Misunderstandings, Chapter 3)

Read

Once you've reworded each section as a question, you can read the material to find an answer. Read only one section at a time so you can make sure you understand it before going on. As you answer a question, don't just rely on material in the text. Think about what you already know from your life experiences and from other classes.

Consider reading in a way that takes advantage of your strongest learning style. If your learning style is visual, highlight as you read, and translate what you read into pictures, drawings and diagrams in the margins or in your notes. If your learning style is aural, consider reading the book aloud, taping it, and then listening to the tape. If you learn best by reading/writing, you'll want to read all of the hand-outs and practice questions provided. If you're a kinesthetic learner, you'll learn by doing the activities on the course website and completing the exercises at the end of each chapter. Review the specific strategies for your learning style presented in the preceding pages and use them.

Recite

After you've read the material, test your understanding by putting the ideas into your own words. Another word for reciting is explaining. Your goal here is to test your knowledge by rewording it. You can do this either in writing or by verbally explaining the material to a study partner, friend, or family member.

Reciting takes many forms; in fact, you'd be wise to use as many senses as you can. Consider using the techniques you learned in the VARK analysis. Are there some methods that work particularly well for your learning style? Now is the time to use them. If you're a visual learner, look up from your reading and recite what you've just learned by picturing the answer. Recall a visual from your notes and turn it into words. If you're an aural learner, speak your knowledge aloud and hear it in your own voice. If your preferred learning style is reading-writing, write the answer in your own words and read it in your own handwriting. If you are a kinesthetic learner, try to use all of your senses. Think of real life experiences and examples of what you're learning; act out concepts by actually practicing the skills in this course in various real situations. Most important in this step is translating information into your own words, not just memorizing someone else's words.

Review

Finally, review what you've learned by creating summarizing statements—either in full sentences or outlines. You can create review documents in short chunks (e.g., sections of a chapter) or on a chapter-by-chapter basis. These review documents can serve you well as you study for exams, so be sure to save them.

SQ3R is not a method to speed up studying like speed-reading techniques, and it is not a method for cramming the night before a final. It is a long-range approach to better understand and retain knowledge learned over the course of the semester. It is a method for studying texts that can help you succeed in this course if applied early and consistently. Learning in small segments and reviewing often results in greater learning and retention than cramming. We have inserted reminders to use this method in each chapter of this *Student Success Manual*.

Additional Study Ideas

Mark Your Texts

Forget the admonitions from your elementary teachers not to mark in your books. Studying is not a passive activity. You want to do more than just read your text; you want to study it, prepare for your exam, and increase your long-term retention of the information. When you mark your text you involve touch and movement, not just vision. This increased activity can stimulate brain activity and recall. Writing side notes to yourself, underlining, circling, and highlighting involve you in the process of learning. Here are some guidelines for marking your texts:

1. **Read before you mark.** In order to figure out what is most important, you need to read a paragraph or section before you mark it up. As you read, try to distinguish main points from details. Analyze as you read to see categories and relationships of ideas. Before you mark, determine what is most important to focus on in order to review and remember.

2. **Develop a code of your own.** You might use circles for thesis statements and underlining for examples. When subpoints are spread out over several pages, you might use one color to highlight items of the same category. Use brackets, parenthesis, underlines, or quotation marks; develop a system that works for you. Improve your ability to spot the key ideas, relationships, causes and effects, and contrasts and similarities. If you need to, write down your code at the beginning of the chapter.

3. **Make notes in the margin.** Summarize a section in a few words of your own. Translate information into your way of talking and relate it to the lecture, another class or your personal life. Create a short outline or drawing in the margin to help you recall or relate information. Annotate for your benefit—do what helps you.

4. **Mark thoughtfully so you don't mark everything.** Marking more than 20 percent of the text defeats the purpose of distinguishing the key information to review later. Read first and think carefully about what to mark.

Choose Your Environment

Choose an effective setting in which to study. A successful study setting has minimal interruptions and distractions from external noise, other people, phones, televisions, and doorbells. A computer may help you take notes, organize your information, create study guides, and focus on the material you're learning or it might distract you with e-mail, instant messages, and surfing. It will take resolve not to answer the phone or check e-mail during your study time. Think about the physical environment of your study location and its comfort in terms of furnishings, lighting, and temperature. Consider furniture that is comfortable, but will not lull you to sleep. Chairs, desks and lighting should give you space and motivation to read and write. Keep the resources you need (paper, pencils, highlighters, dictionary) but not a lot more. Once you identify a place that works well for you to study, train yourself to use that place often so your brain associates serious study with that location. College libraries usually have well-designed, well-lit spaces with minimal distractions. The Study Environment Analysis (www.ucc.vt.edu/stdysk/ studydis.html) allows you to analyze study settings to determine the best environment for you.

Attend Study Sessions

If your professor or TA announces a study session, make it a priority to attend. These small sessions provide opportunities to review and ask questions. If study sessions are not sponsored by your professor, form a study group with other dedicated students. Talking through the material, reviewing each other's notes, and quizzing each other will enhance your study skills and your comprehension and retention of the course concepts.

Seek Help

Familiarize yourself with your campus tutoring centers and labs, study skills workshops, student success centers, communication labs, supplemental instruction, peer mentoring, learning support services, learning assistance centers, or student learning centers. Check out resources to assist you in studying, writing assignments, and preparing for exams.

If you have a learning difficulty or disability, locate and use available services. The Office of Student Services (or the Office of Special Services) provides screening, diagnosing, and assistance for students with learning difficulties or special needs. If you already have documentation of a special need, take that to the appropriate office to receive services more quickly. If you think you may have dyslexia, Attention Deficit / Hyperactivity Disorder (ADHD), or any learning disability, you can arrange for a professional screening. After the screening, you can be referred for further testing or to other services to meet your needs. If you ask, colleges usually provide note-takers, books on tape, additional time for tests, and other reasonable accommodations for special needs.

Taking Notes in Class

The previous section offered advice for studying on your own. This section will help you understand the material that your professor presents in class. In addition to using the approaches for class lectures, you can also use them as a supplement or alternative to the SQ3R approach for better understanding the text and other readings. Two popular methods of note taking are the Cornell format and mind maps.

Cornell Note-Taking System

Taking notes while reading or while listening to a lecture occupies much of your time as a student. One tried-and-true method of note taking is the Cornell system. You can utilize this system with the following steps:

1. Before you begin to take notes, draw a vertical line down the left side of your paper about a fourth of the way over (2" from the left on an 8½" x 11" page).

2. As you listen for main points (see Chapter 4's section on informational listening), take notes on the right side.

3. Later, as you review your notes, put key words, significant phrases, and sample questions in the left column.

SAMPLE: Cornell Note-Taking System

2. Second, pull out key words and phrases and create questions here.	**1. First, take notes on this side. Leave space to add to notes from text or readings. Focus on big ideas.**
Group Interdependent What size is a small group?	Groups are collections of individuals that interact over time and are interdependent. Usually between 3 and 20 people.
Hidden agenda	Group members have common goals. Individual goals not shared with the group are called hidden agendas. (One person wants to make connections to get a new job—something just for him—but the group goal is to complete a report.)

Mind Mapping

Mind mapping is a technique you can use to take notes from a lecture or text and improve your recall of the ideas. A mind map is a visual representation of the material that emphasizes relationships of concepts. While an outline emphasizes linear relationships, a mind map (also called a concept map) shows associations, links and connections in a holistic way. An outline is more like a book; a mind map resembles information assembled as web links. Visual learners especially benefit from this method.

To construct your mind map, follow these guidelines:

1. Start in the middle of a large unlined sheet of paper.

2. Use only key words not sentences.

3. Use images (arrows, circles, sketches) that help you recall ideas and show relationships between words and groups of words.

4. Use colors to link related ideas and separate others.

5. Be creative.

A mind map of a lecture on listening might look like this:

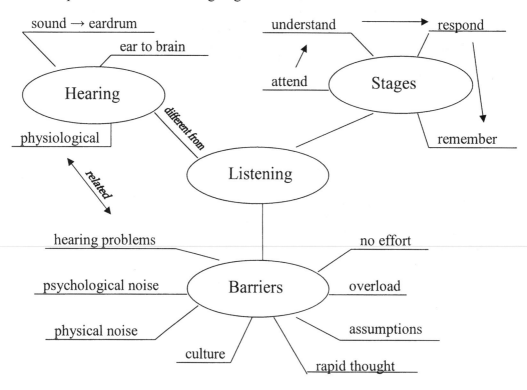

TEST-TAKING SKILLS

In most of your classes, you will take exams. Whether these are short, five-question quizzes or two-hour essay exams, here are some tips to improve your exam scores.

1. **Prepare for the exam you'll be given.** Read the syllabus carefully or talk with your instructor to find out what types of exams you'll take. Your text, this *Student Success Manual*, and the *Understanding Human Communication* website provide many tools to study for different kinds of exams. Ideally, you'll know the material well enough to be able to pass any type of exam; practically, you can use your time and energy to prepare most efficiently if you know the type of exam you'll be faced with. Here are some pointers for three common types of exam questions.

True/False

A. If the *whole* sentence isn't true, it isn't true. Conversely, if any part is false, it is false. Don't be thrown off by a partial truth buried in an otherwise false statement. Look for any falsehood.

B. Be aware of absolutes (always, never, only) and remember that if there is one exception, the question is false.

C. Statements phrased with negatives can be confusing. If changing it to a positive makes it true, the original sentence phrased as a negative is generally false. For example, "Nonverbal communication cannot be used to deceive." If you make this sentence a positive, it becomes "Nonverbal communication can be used to deceive." Since this is true, the opposite of the sentence must be false.

Multiple Choice

A. Read the first part of the question and think of the answer you would give if no choices were provided. Then see if that is one of the choices.

B. Before marking the answer, read all choices to be sure yours is the best. Most multiple-choice directions say choose the **best** answer, so all choices may be somewhat correct, but one might be better than the others. For instance, if you are choosing the best paraphrase, and one choice only paraphrases thoughts and another choice only paraphrases feelings, look for a *best* answer that paraphrases both thoughts and feelings. If a choice is more complete than others, it may be the best choice, even though others may be technically correct.

C. Check if "all (or none) of the above" is a choice. If you know for sure that two or three choices are correct (or incorrect), consider the "all (none) of the above" option.

D. Negative questions can be confusing. If the question is worded as a negative look at each option and mentally change the question to a positive. Then mark each choice that works. Generally, you will mark all but one and that one will be the correct answer for the original (negative) question. For example, "Which of the following is **not** a function of nonverbal communication?" can be mentally changed to "Which of these **is** a function of nonverbal communication?" If all but one choice correctly answers the second question, the unmarked question will generally be your answer to the original question.

E. If two choices seem too similar, re-read the question to be sure you understand what the question asks. Check carefully for some small difference in the answers, making one a better choice. Perhaps neither is correct; see if there is a better answer altogether.

Essay

A. Familiarize yourself with the types of words used in essays and be sure you understand their meaning. Commonly used words are describe, review, explain, compare, contrast, discuss, and evaluate. For each word, the instructor looks for a different reasoning process and type of answer. Read the question carefully and mark the words that tell you what type of answer is expected. Familiarize yourself with the definitions of twenty commonly used words found in essay questions at   http://www.studygs.net/essayterms.htm

B. Create an initial outline for each answer. Jot down an outline for each question, organizing your ideas around major themes that answer the question. State your thesis and your support. While you are writing one answer, if an idea pops into your head for another question, quickly add it to the outline.

C. Divide your time so that you answer each question. Your professor may give you partial credit for an outline or some sentences that show you understand the material, even if the grammar isn't correct and the thoughts aren't complete. Leaving a ten-point question blank results in losing ten points, no matter how extensive your answer to another question is.

D. Write neatly with space between your lines. This will allow you to go back and add information you think of later. If you are writing and you know the concept but can't think of the precise term or name, leave a blank, describe it, and fill it in later. You may think of it later or find it used in another part of the exam.

2. **Predict and prepare for likely types of test questions.** Use the outline provided in this *Student Success Manual* and the more extensive one in the *Study Guide* on the course website to predict objective questions. For instance, if there are four steps or three characteristics listed, be prepared for a multiple-choice question that asks, "Which one of these is . . ." or "Which one of these is not . . ." Creating an outline or mind map from your lecture notes will help you predict questions on that material.

3. **Use practice questions effectively**. Use the course website to practice multiple-choice, true/false, fill-in-the-blank, and matching questions. Use this *Student Success Manual* to study for short-answer and synthesis questions. When using sample questions with an answer key, don't look at the answer key while answering the questions. If you simply tell yourself (after seeing the correct answer), "Yes, that's the answer I would have chosen," then using the sample exams will not benefit you. Take the sample exams as actual exams without looking at the answers. Then go back and actually grade yourself. This reveals gaps in your knowledge and helps redirect your study time more productively.

4. **Arrive rested, early, and relaxed**. Be sure you've slept and eaten. Be comfortable and settled before the exam is handed out, with any necessary pens, pencils, and blue books at hand. Put away any unnecessary items so you're not distracted. If you can, relax your body by taking a few slow, deep breaths. Anxiety produces a body on "alert" that is not as capable of test taking as a calmer body.

5. **Plan your time.** Know how much each section of the exam is worth and then set up a time frame for yourself so you'll be able to spend the appropriate amount of time on each section. Check your time to be sure you're staying on task. If there is no penalty for guessing, then guess.

6. **Begin with what you know**. Peruse the exam and jot down ideas for questions you'll answer later. Then begin with the easy questions first to build confidence and get in the swing of things.

7. **Use the hints the exam provides.** Read carefully. Often the answer to one question is contained in another question. Stay alert to information that might be given. If one question is "List and describe the twelve major categories of Jack Gibb's theory of supportive and defensive communication" and another question is "Jack Gibb is best known for his theory of _____," the answer to the second is contained in the first.

8. **Analyze your exam to prepare for the next one.** Always learn from one exam so you can improve on the next one. An exam analysis is provided on the next page. Complete the exam analysis before you talk with your instructor and take it with you; it shows that you are serious about learning from exams, not just grubbing for points.

Postexam Analysis

After your exam, go through the exam and note the number of each item you missed, the code for the type of question you missed, the code for the reason you missed it, and any additional information that is important.

Come up with a plan to improve your studying and your exam scores.

Code for types of questions missed:		
MC = Multiple Choice	**T/F** = True, False	**SA** = Short Answer
E = Essay	**FB** = Fill in the Blank	**M** = Matching

Code for reasons I missed items:
AB = Absent the day it was covered.
NN = Not in my notes, although I was there and took notes when it was explained.
N = It was in my notes, but I didn't study or comprehend it.
T = Answer was in the text; I didn't read it or didn't remember it.
MRQ = I misread the question. (reading error)
MUQ = I read the question but misunderstood what was asked. (comprehension error)
V = I didn't understand some of the general vocabulary used to ask the question.
DRC = I didn't read all choices; I picked one I thought was right without reading all.
H = I hurried to get to the end.
RCW = I had it right, erased it, and changed it to a wrong answer.

# Exam question missed	Code for type of question	Code for reason I missed the question	Additional, important information about the question or answer

Now go through your columns and see if you can determine a pattern. Did you miss mostly one type of question? Seek help for answering that type of question. Did you miss questions for one particular reason? What can you do to rectify that?

Write a paragraph in which you summarize what you learn from this analysis and create, in list or paragraph format, a plan to improve the skills you need to do better on the next exam.

WRITING

In addition to study and test-taking skills, your grades in college often hinge on your writing assignments. You've been learning to write for years, and in college it is especially important to apply all you've learned. Successful writing depends on your planning, development, organization, avoidance of plagiarism, and mastery of writing mechanics.

Planning

Read the assignment carefully and ask about anything you don't understand. Underline words on the assignment sheet that give requirements or planning details. Know the required length of the paper. Begin by clarifying your purpose so you know exactly why you are writing and who your audience is. Understand whether you are being asked to express an opinion, prove a point, analyze a situation, synthesize research, apply a theory, summarize an article, or accomplish some other purpose. Personal response or application papers are very different from book summaries, abstracts, or research papers. Determine whether your paper will be read only by your professor, by a panel, or by classmates as well. If you first know your purpose and your audience, you can plan more successfully. Write down your audience and purpose, and then sketch out a tentative thesis, outline, and possible supporting materials. See the step-by-step advice for planning major papers in "Timeline for a Term Paper" at the end of this section.

Development

Short opinion or analysis papers may not require outside research. They will, however, require that you develop your thoughts and support for your ideas carefully, but not necessarily with outside research. You will improve your development of any paper if you clarify your understanding of the types, functions, and styles of support explained in Chapter 11 of *Understanding Human Communication* ("Supporting Material"). While writing and speaking differ, the underlying principles and guidelines will serve you well in developing the types of support most appropriate to your paper. Whether you need to check a few facts or conduct extensive research, "Gathering Information" in Chapter 10 will help you develop your paper by using search engines, evaluating Web sites, and conducting library research.

Organization

Whether preparing papers or speeches, you'll do well to follow the guidelines for organization presented in Chapter 11 of *Understanding Human Communication*. Start with a thesis statement and carefully organize your main points and subpoints in a logical pattern. (See "Principles of Outlining" and "Organizing Your Points in a Logical Order.") Then structure your supporting material coherently for greatest impact. Use transitions in your paper as you would in a speech, to help readers understand the direction of your paper and how what you've already said relates to what comes next. (See "Using Transitions.") Finally, when your paper is largely written and you see your creation as a whole, it is time to write an introductory paragraph that gets the readers' attention, states the thesis, and previews the main points. Then write your conclusion so it reviews your thesis and main points and creates closure. Looking at the introduction and conclusion side by side helps you see whether your paper has unity and cohesion. (See "Beginning and Ending the Speech.")

Plagiarism

Virtually every student knows that cheating is a grave academic offense. Nobody who copies answers from a stolen test or a friend can claim ignorance of the rules as a defense. Plagiarism, though, isn't as well understood. Read your college's code of conduct or code of academic integrity to see its definition of academic dishonesty and plagiarism. Here is a breakdown of the most widely recognized types of plagiarism.

Copying

Replicating another person's work word-for-word is plagiarism. This includes any format or activity that involves taking someone else's work (for example, their paper, speech, cartoon, or exam) and presenting it as your own in any form (report, speech, or paper). If you are quoting someone else directly in writing, indicate their words in quotation marks and properly cite the source. An English handbook will show you how to do citations. In speaking, use an oral citation to clarify the words and the source. Sometimes, plagiarism results from hurried or careless research if you later cannot determine whether your note cards contain a summary in your own words or quotations from your source. Avoid this by consistently using quotation marks appropriately and carefully coding your notes.

Paraphrasing

Even if you put others' writings in your own words, you must credit the source. If the words are largely your own paraphrase, but include key words and phrases from another source, put the key words and phrases in quotation marks and cite the source.

Using ideas

Even though you are not quoting or paraphrasing, credit the source of an idea. The exception is information that is common knowledge and is found without credits in multiple quality sources. For instance, almost all communication texts list many types of nonverbal communication, including a category about how far or close we interact with each other. This category, called proxemics, is common knowledge and needs no citations. However, if you describe the distances at which we interact as "intimate, personal, social, and public," those are the words and ideas of Edward T. Hall, and his work would need to be cited.[1]

---

[1] E. Hall, *The Hidden Dimension* (Garden City, NY: Anchor Books, 1969).

Drawing on non-print sources

The basis of your writing might be a movie, television show, radio broadcast, or Web site. If ideas, paraphrases, or quotations come from these, be sure to cite them. Style guides and English handbooks give you formats for doing so.

In brief, credit those who shape your research and ideas. In the process, your citations demonstrate that you've researched and studied beyond your text. You get credit for researching and enhance your credibility when you cite quality work. Be sure to do your own synthesizing, analyzing, and reflecting on your research so that your thesis and writing reflects your own thinking and is not just a series of quotations strung together. The ideas, organization, and particular process of asking and answering a research question should be yours. Demonstrate that you have original thoughts, interpretations, analyses, and means of expression supported by current research and experts.

Grammar and Mechanics

No matter how brilliant your thoughts are, grammatical and mechanical errors create "noise" for the grader so that your ideas get lost. Use complete sentences to create coherent paragraphs. A spelling and grammar check on your computer helps, but it misses many types of errors, so don't rely solely on it. Use the online and in-person resources available to you to review grammar and spelling concerns. After you proofread, have a tutor or competent friend read your paper to see if it makes sense, is readable, and is free of errors. Double-check that your paper adheres to specific requirements with regard to acceptable font style and size, spacing, margins, and style (APA or MLA).

Checklist for Your Paper

Reviewing this checklist might improve your paper and your grade. Does your paper:

☐ get your readers' attention in the opening paragraph?

☐ state your thesis and preview your main points in your opening paragraph?

☐ present ideas in an organized and logical manner?

☐ sound coherent? Do ideas make sense and hang together?

☐ have a topic sentence in each paragraph and other complete sentences that logically follow to make a point?

☐ develop ideas with adequate support for the points made?

☐ use transitions to help the reader understand the movement from one idea to another?

☐ have an interesting and summative conclusion that reviews the main points and brings closure?

☐ use the required sources (kind and number)?

☐ cite all sources in the proper style?

☐ mark direct quotations appropriately?

☐ credit paraphrases and ideas of others?

☐ have no spelling and grammar errors?

☐ include a cover page (if required) with title, your name, professor's name, course number and section, and date?

☐ conform to the deadline?

☐ adhere to requirements for length, spacing, fonts, and any additional instructions on the assignment sheet?

Timeline for a Term Paper

Putting off a writing assignment is a plan for disaster. It's not likely that you can put together a decent paper if you start a day or two before the deadline. Use a calendar or day planner to plot the day the assignment is due and then work backward to design a workable timeline of activities needed to complete the paper. For a term paper, create a semester plan. Adjust your timetable accordingly for shorter writing assignments that may not require as much research. Always allow time to revise and rewrite. The Assignment Calculator (www.lib.umn.edu/help/calculator) prompts you to plug in the date your paper is due and displays a day-planner guide to work on this assignment. Each step of the way you can click on tools to help you organize your thoughts, create a plan, and locate detailed tips.

As you proceed, save your work frequently, and always make a copy of your work so you never lose all of it. Too many students have learned this lesson the hard way with a low grade to prove it.

For a research paper due the 14th week of the term, your timeline might look like this:

Weeks 2 – 3

✓ **Know your assignment**. Read the assignment carefully and ask questions if you are not sure what the process and the final product should look like.

✓ **Update your research skills**. Students are often unaware of the resources in their university library. What resources—journals, books, databases, special collections —do you have access to? Don't think you have to discover these on your own: Get to know the reference librarian and ask for help.

✓ **Choose your topic.** If the professor is assigning topics, get yours as early as you can. If there is a list to choose from, pick yours early. If the topic is your choice, make sure your instructor agrees that it fits the assignment. See Chapter 10 of *Understanding Human Communication* for advice on choosing a topic. When you've identified a likely topic, do a quick search to see if there seems to be enough information. Narrow your topic. Make sure it fits the assigned length of the project.

Weeks 4 – 5

✓ **Develop a research question** that specifically asks the question you are trying to answer through your research. Careful wording of the question helps you organize and plan your research and, later, your writing.

✓ **Clarify the kinds of research required**. Professors may allow only scholarly (peer-reviewed) journals or may require a certain number or percentage be scholarly. The number and type of web sites allowed may be limited. Know before you begin so you use your time wisely.

✓ **Devise your research strategy** by working with a reference librarian to find the information you need. Ask about indexes, catalogs, databases, and Internet resources. Keep records of the sources (databases, key words, Web sites) you've researched so you don't duplicate your efforts.

✓ **Critically review and evaluate your sources**. See Web references in the Internet Resources section to help you with this.

✓ **Take notes and create a working outline.** Careful notes help you avoid plagiarism and clarify what is or isn't another person's work. Be consistent with a system to identify whether you have exact quotes, paraphrases, or ideas from another person.

✓ **Record your sources in the required format** so that you can properly cite them in your references or works cited list. Know what style is required for your final paper and cite your sources in that format now. This saves hours of backtracking later to find a part of the citation you'd forgotten. Most communication courses will use APA or MLA styles; references for both are in the Internet Resources section on page 31.

✓ **Broaden or narrow your topic** depending on the amount of information you find.

Weeks 7 – 9

✓ **Create a thesis statement and outline**. When you have much of the information you need, develop a thesis and main points in complete sentences and note where your research will be inserted to develop your points. Your outline helps you see what pieces of information are missing and what sections require more research.

✓ **Continue your research** to round out your paper.

Weeks 10 – 11

✓ **Begin writing** when you have all of your information and your outline. As you write, focus on answering your research question.

✓ **Follow the technical requirements** for the paper. Read the assignment or check with the professor to be certain about the spacing, font size, margins, style (APA or MLA), and cover required.

✓ **Revise and rewrite.** Allow time to seek help from your professor, TA, writing lab, or tutor. Be certain to print a hard copy and create a backup of everything at this point. Back up your work each time you revise.

Weeks 12 – 13

✓ **Proofread**. Ask others to read your paper for coherence and errors.

✓ **Finish** your paper at least two days before the due date to allow for computer crashes and printer problems. Print a copy and proofread the hard copy. This also guarantees having something in hand should you experience a technology failure.

CLASSROOM CIVILITY

You'll be more successful in this and other classes if you accept the responsibilities that come with being a student.

1. **Know the rules of the course.** Check your syllabus; it generally spells out what you can expect in the class and what's expected of you. Since no two classes have identical rules, you can save yourself grief and boost the odds of success by investing time in reading that syllabus. Some professors even give a pop quiz on the contents of the syllabus.

2. **Attend each class.** Attendance plays an important part in college success and students who don't skip class have several advantages: they hear explanations of assignments and changes in assignments, due dates, or test dates. They hear test reviews, they can ask questions, and they often gain an edge if a grade is borderline. Attendance attests to your seriousness as a student and your willingness to take responsibility for your learning. In a communication class such as this, participation in class activities often accounts for both learning the skills and is part of the assessment (grade) for the course.

3. **Show up on time**. In some cultures and some high schools, being tardy is accepted, but the culture of college classrooms is that classes start on time and you're tardy (or marked absent) if you're not there for the start of class.

4. **Come prepared**. Check the syllabus and be sure you read the assigned chapters before class. You'll be prepared for quizzes, activities based on the reading, and lectures. You'll also understand more from the lectures.

5. **Accept responsibility: What you do (and don't do).** If you're absent from a class, find out what you missed from your professor or other students before the next meeting and do what's necessary to stay caught up. If the syllabus clearly tells you to check the Web site and not to contact the professor to find out what you've missed, follow that advice. Turn in work on time. If an assignment is late, acknowledge that fact. Excuses usually won't impress your professor, who has probably heard them all before.

   Another way to accept responsibility is to avoid the "you" language described in Chapter 7. For example, instead of attacking your professor by saying, "You didn't explain this very well," use "I" language and say, "I didn't understand . . ."

6. **Behave in a civil manner.** Since you don't want to antagonize your professor and fellow students, follow the basic rules of civil behavior in groups. Show up on time to class. Turn off your cell phone and pager. Don't hold side conversations or butt into a lecture or discussion without being recognized first.

7. **Show your interest.** Even if you aren't constantly fascinated by what's happening in class, acting the part of an interested student will make a good impression; and often acting interested may even help you feel more engaged. Nonverbal indicators that you are interested include leaning forward, making eye contact, smiling, nodding responsively and appropriately, asking sincere and thoughtful questions, and volunteering for activities if

asked. These behaviors will likely enhance your own learning and that of your classmates. In addition, you will help to create a supportive classroom climate.

Ask questions. If you don't understand, ask. Ask in a way that does not create defensiveness or take unnecessary class time. If something has been explained, try to identify the specific point you don't understand, rather than ask for the whole topic to be repeated. Specific questions, such as asking the professor to differentiate between two points, "Could you explain when self-concept and self-esteem are different?" or asking for an example, "Could you give an example of how self-concept and self-esteem differ?" will help you more than a general request like, "Can you go over self-concept and self-esteem again?" As you study, prepare questions that delve deeper into the material, questions that will help you understand. If you feel uncomfortable or if there is no opportunity to ask in class, try to ask the professor after class, during office hours, or by e-mail. The important thing is to ask.

Avoid behaviors that say you're *not* interested in class: text-messaging, reading another book, talking, rummaging through your pack or purse, putting your head down, sleeping, and so forth. You get the picture.

8. **Treat others with respect in class discussions.** Listen to other points of view. Part of classroom civility is hearing and responding appropriately to others' opinions. Classrooms are marketplaces of ideas; prepare to hear and listen to opinions different from yours.

Understand others before responding. Before you respond to someone else, be sure you've understood his or her point of view. Use perception checks (Chapter 2) and paraphrases (Chapter 4) to clarify what the other has said before you respond. Use these skills to ensure that you don't embarrass yourself with a lengthy disagreement, only to find that you misunderstood the point.

In your own comments, avoid acting dogmatically when you are actually expressing your opinion. Rather than saying, "Women are . . ." or "Men are . . .," use the phrase, "In my opinion, women are . . ." or "In my experience, men are . . ." This shows you understand the difference between facts, opinions, and inferences—concepts covered in Chapter 3. Other phrases that can help you be clear about recognizing that what you are saying is your own opinion, not absolute fact, are "I have learned . . .," "I have come to believe . . .," "I am convinced . . .," or "I have concluded . . ." This sort of language is less likely to trigger defensiveness than dogmatic statements. You can help reduce defensiveness and build a positive communication climate (Chapter 7).

9. **Stay positive**. Approach the class with a positive attitude and, even when frustrated, don't take your frustration out on the professor or other students. Stating that you're frustrated is okay but unnecessary. Stating, "I want to be sure I understand this. I want to learn this" are positive affirmations for you, your professor, and your classmates. You will generally get a more positive reaction than if you begin on a negative note like, "This is really hard. I don't know how you expect us to remember all these key terms." Focus on your goals. If your goal is to learn and to understand, stay focused on that. For more details about positive thinking benefits for students, see www.marin.cc.ca.us/~don/Study/Hcontents.html.

10. **Recognize that success takes work.** Joining a class is like signing up for a gym membership; even though you're a "customer," you will only benefit if you follow the plan your coach (i.e., your professor) sets out for you. Commit to showing up for your classes (workouts) ready to do what it takes to tone up your understanding.

How well are you doing? Use the Classroom Savvy Checklist to find out: www.mtsu.edu/~studskl/savylist.htm.

INTERNET RESOURCES

Attention Deficit Disorder

Causes, characteristics, treatment, and legal issues plus strategies for coping, studying, and learning: www.ucc.vt.edu/stdysk/addhandbook.html

Attitude

www.marin.cc.ca.us/~don/Study/Hcontents.html

Avoiding Plagiarism

http://gervaseprograms.georgetown.edu/honor/system/53377.html
www.indiana.edu/~wts/pamphlets/plagiarism.shtml

Classroom Savvy Checklist

www.mtsu.edu/~studskl/savylist.htm

Cornell Note Taking

www.bucks.edu/~specpop/Cornl-ex.htm

Evaluating Sources

http://owl.english.purdue.edu/workshops/hypertext/EvalSrcW/index.html

Learning Styles

www.vark-learn.com

Marking Texts

http://www.utexas.edu/student/utlc/learning_resources/reading/Mark_Your_Books.pdf

Mind and Concept Mapping

How to mind map with sample: www.mindtools.com/mindmaps.html
How to mind map: www.peterussell.com/MindMaps/HowTo.html
Outline/example of mind mapping: www.bucks.edu/~specpop/sem-map.htm
Examples of web, tree, chart, chain, sketch:
     www.bucks.edu/~specpop/vis-org-ex.htm#web

Concept mapping:

    www.utc.edu/Administration/WalkerTeachingResourceCenter/FacultyDevelopment/ConceptMapping/index.html#what-is

Concept mapping homepage: http://users.edte.utwente.nl/lanzing/cm_home.htm

Overcoming Procrastination

http://www.utexas.edu/student/utlc/learning_resources/motivation_procrastination/Overcoming_Procrastination.pdf

SQ3R

www.studygs.net/texred2.htm
www.arc.sbc.edu/sq3r.html
www.teach-nology.com/web_tools/graphic_org/sq3r/

Test-Taking Skills

http://www.studygs.net/essayterms.htm

Writing Assistance

www.ucc.vt.edu/stdysk/termpapr.html
http://webster.commnet.edu/mla/index.shtml
http://owl.english.purdue.edu/handouts/index.html

Writing Papers

www.lib.umn.edu/help/calculator

Writing Styles

APA: www.wisc.edu/writetest/Handbook/DocAPAReferences.html
MLA: http://webster.commnet.edu/mla/index.shtml

Chapter 1: Interpersonal Process

SQ3R in Action

Generate an SQ3R chart for this chapter here:
http://www.teach-nology.com/web_tools/graphic_org/sq3r

Survey

Skim the title, key terms, chapter outline, objectives ("You should understand" and "You should be able to"), headings, tables, photos, cartoons, figures, charts, and items in the margin. Glance at the titles of the Focus on Research, Reflection, Film Clips, Self-Assessment, and Dark Side. At the end of each chapter, look over the Summary, Critical Thinking Probes, Ethical Challenges, Skill Builder, and Resources.

Question

Ask yourself questions. What do you know about these topics from your own life experiences and from other classes? Ask these six questions in each section: who, what, when, where, how, and why?

Read

Take one heading at a time and read to find the answers to the questions you've posed.

Recite

In your own words, say the answer aloud and then write it out.

Review

Review each section and then review the whole chapter. This is a good time to use the activities at the end of each chapter and the activities and the sample exams on the course website. Remember to periodically review the previous chapters as well.

Chapter 1: Outline

(Italicized words are key terms.)

I. Why we communicate—All humans have a need to communicate, as satisfying relationships can literally be a matter of life and death, and while not everyone needs the same amount of contact, personal communication is essential for physical well-being.
    A. Identity needs are met through communication, which is the major way we learn who we are as humans, as we enter the world with little or no sense of identity and only gain one by the way others define us.
    B. Social needs are met through communication, as it is the principle way relationships are created.

    C. Practical needs are met through communication every day, as it serves important functions.

II.   The Communication Process—Human communication is a complex process with many components.

    A.   Communication theorists develop sophisticated *transactional communication models* in an attempt to depict all the factors that affect human interaction.

    B.   The communication model replaces the roles of sender and receiver (which can be impossible to distinguish) with the term "communicator."

        1.   Meanings exist in and among peoples' messages, verbal or nonverbal; these messages do not have inherent meanings, because meanings reside in the people who express and interpret them.

        2.   *Feedback* indicates a response to the previous message.

        3.   Environment and noise affect communication.

            a.   *Environments* are fields of experience that help people make sense of others' behavior.

            b.   *Noise* is anything that interferes with the transmission and reception of a message.

                i.   *External* noise includes different kinds of distractions that are outside the receiver that make it difficult to hear.

                ii.   *Physiological* noise involves biological factors that interfere with reception.

                iii.   *Psychological* noise refers to cognitive factors that lessen the effectiveness of communication.

        4.   Channels make a difference, as *channels* are the medium through which messages are exchanged, and the selection of the channel depends in part on the kind of message that is being sent.

    C.   Communication Principles—In addition to the insights of the communication model, there are other principles that guide understanding of communication.

        1.   Communication is transactional; communication is a dynamic process that the participants create through their interaction with one another.

        2.   Communication can be intentional or unintentional, as all behavior has communicative value.

        3.   Communication has a content and a relational dimension. The *content dimension* involves the information being explicitly discussed, while the *relational dimension* expresses how you feel about the other person.

        4.   Communication is irreversible; it is impossible to "unreceive" a message, as words and deeds, once said or done, are irretrievable.

        5.   Communication is unrepeatable, because the same words and behavior are different each time they are spoken or performed.

    D.   Communication misconceptions—Avoiding these common misconceptions can save you trouble in your personal life.

        1.   Not all communication seeks understanding. It is a flawed assumption that the goal of all communication is to maximize

understanding between communicators; instead, social rituals we enact every day attempt to influence others. Deliberate ambiguity and deception are examples of communication in which understanding is not the primary goal.

2.   More communication is not always better, as excessive communication is unproductive or even aggravates a problem; there are times when no interaction is the best course of action.

3.   Communication will not solve all problems, because even best-timed and best-planned communication cannot fix all problems.

4.   Effective communication is not a natural ability, because most people operate at a level of effectiveness far below their potential.

III.   Interpersonal communication defined: Some types of communication are uniquely interpersonal.

A.   *Quantitative and qualitative* definitions of interpersonal communication have been defined in the following ways:

1.   Quantitative definitions of interpersonal communication are based on the number of participants (which is two—called a *dyad*) and the terms "dyadic communication" and "interpersonal communication" may be used interchangeably since they are both interaction between two people, which is different than group interaction.

2.   Qualitative definitions are based on the quality and nature of the interpersonal relationship, not the number of participants.

B.   Most relationships fall somewhere between personal and impersonal.

IV.   Technological changes have given us new options for communicating personally, including *computer-mediated communication* (CMC), which includes e-mail, texting, instant messaging, social networking, and blogging.

A.   Computer-mediated communication can increase both the amount and the quality of interpersonal communication, since it is easier than face-to-face communication.

B.   There are challenges of mediated communication; *richness* describes the abundance of nonverbal cues that add clarity to a verbal message, which is missing from most mediated communication, making for leaner messages.

1.   *Disinhibition* is the tendency to transmit messages without considering the consequence. This can take two forms: volunteering of personal information that might normally not be expressed, and messages that may be more direct in a critical way than in face-to-face contact.

C.   It is a challenge to choose the best communication channel, as each channel has both pros and cons.

V.   Research has identified a great deal of important and useful information about communication.

A.   *Communication competence* is defined as communication that is both effective and appropriate.

1.   There is no single ideal or effective way to communicate. The definition of what communication is appropriate in a given situation varies considerably from one culture to another.

2.   Competence is situational, as communication competence is not absolute but exists in degrees or areas of competence.

3.   Competence can be learned; it is a set of skills that anyone can learn.

B.   There are several common characteristics that characterize effective communication in most contexts.

1.   A large repertoire of skills can help communicators achieve a variety of goals.

2.   In addition to having a large repertoire, one must be adaptable and able to choose the right one for the situation.

3.   Once you have chosen the appropriate way to communicate, you must practice to become skillful.

4.   Effective communication occurs when the people are involved and care about one another and about the topic at hand.

5.   Empathy/perspective taking is the ability to understand and influence others.

6.   *Cognitive complexity* is the ability to construct a variety of different frameworks for viewing an issue.

7.   *Self-monitoring* describes the process of paying close attention to one's own behavior and using these observations to shape the way one behaves; this generally increases one's effectiveness as a communicator.

Chapter 1: Summary

We communicate for three reasons: for our physical, social, and practical needs. While competent communication is important, it is not a natural ability, so it must be learned and practiced.

Human communication is a complex process with many components that theorists explain by creating different models representing the process. The most sophisticated, transactional communication models, attempt to show all of the factors that affect human interaction. Several insights have come from this model which include: sending and receiving are usually simultaneous, meanings exist in and among people, environment and noise affect communication, and channels make a difference. Environments are fields of experience that help people make sense of others' behavior. Noise is anything that interferes with the transmission and reception of a message. And the channel is the medium through which messages are exchanged.

Other principles that guide our understanding of communication include: communication is transactional, communication can be either intentional or unintentional, communication has a content and a relational dimension, communication is irreversible, and communication is unrepeatable. The content dimension involves the information being explicitly discussed, and the relational dimension expresses feelings about the other person.

There are some common misconceptions about communication. Namely, not all communication seeks understanding, more communication is not always better, communication will not solve all problems, and effective communication is not a natural ability.

Interpersonal communication can be defined in two different ways, either by taking a quantitative approach or a qualitative approach. A quantitative approach defines interpersonal communication by the number of people in the interaction and regards a dyad, or two persons interacting, as interpersonal, regardless of the type of interaction that is occurring. A qualitative approach, however, focuses on the quality of the interaction to determine if it can be considered interpersonal (e.g., an impersonal professional exchange is obviously not the same communication as a heart-to-heart talk with a friend).

Relationships are made up of personal and impersonal elements. Communication with strangers or non-friends can sometimes become personal, while partners can experience a blend of impersonal and personal communication that varies, depending on the stage of their relationships.

Technological advances have changed how people are able to communicate with one another. Computer-mediated communication (CMC) provides various ways to interact, including e-mail, blogs, text messages, instant messaging, and social networking. The research on the effectiveness of CMC is divided, with some critics arguing that the Internet discourages a sense of community; whereas other researchers have found that the quantity and quality of interpersonal communication increases with the use of CMC.

There are several challenges related to CMC. Face-to-face communication allows for an abundance of nonverbal cues that add clarity to a message, called richness. CMC is missing this component, and as a result the messages are leaner, making them harder to interpret. Another challenge is that, without nonverbal cues, online communicators can create unrealistic images of one another, which encourages "hyperpersonal" communication. Disinhibition often occurs, which is transmitting messages without considering their consequence, either by volunteering inappropriate personal information or being unduly harsh in communicating.

Communication competence includes the ability to be both effective and appropriate in one's communication, and there are many types of competent communication. Competence is situational and learned, but there are several common factors in effective communication. Good communicators have a large repertoire of skills so they can choose the best one for the situation at hand. The communicator must be adaptable, however, and be able to choose the right message. Once the message and channel are chosen, the communicator must be skillful. Involvement with the other person makes for more effective communication. Understanding another's point of view and having empathy offer the best chance at developing an effective message. Cognitive complexity is the ability to construct a variety of different frameworks for viewing an issue. Possessing a large number of constructs for interpreting the behavior of others increases the chances of acting in ways that will produce satisfying results. Self-monitoring is the process of paying close attention to one's own behavior and using those observations to shape the way one behaves.

Chapter 1: Key Terms

For each of these terms, define the term, give an example, and explain the significance of the term.

1. Channel

2. Cognitive complexity

3. Communication competence

4. Computer-mediated communication (CMC)

5. Content dimension (of a message)

6. Dyad

7. Disinhibition

8. Environment

9. Feedback

10. Noise (external, physiological, and psychological)

11. Qualitative interpersonal communication

12. Quantitative interpersonal communication

13. Relational dimension (of a message)

14. Richness (of communication media)

15. Self-monitoring

16. Transactional communication model

Chapter 1: Review Questions

These questions are designed to help you better understand the concepts from this chapter and also allow you the opportunity to put the information into your own words. For practice true/false and multiple-choice questions, please refer to the course website.

1. What are the three needs that are met through communication?

2. Identify and explain the five principles of communication.

3. What are four commonly held misconceptions about communication?

4. What are two ways that interpersonal communication can be defined?

5. What is communication competence?

Chapter 1: Thinking Outside the Box: Synthesizing Your Knowledge

These questions are designed to help connect the course material from previous chapters.

1. Identify some of the nonverbal cues (Chapter 6) that are missing from computer-mediated communication (CMC), thus making the messages leaner.

2. Explain one of the forms that disinhibition can take in computer-mediated communication (CMC) and the possible impact it might have on the relationship between communicators (Chapter 3).

Chapter 1: Answers to Review Questions

1. What are the three needs that are met through communication?

   Identity needs are how we learn who we are; as humans we enter the world with little or no sense of identity that develops as others define us. Social needs are met through communication,n as it is the principle way relationships are created. Practical needs are met through communication every day, as it serves important functions.

2. Identify and explain the five principles of communication.

   Communication is transactional, meaning that it is a dynamic process that the participants create through their interaction with one another. Communication can be intentional or unintentional, as all behavior has communicative value. Communication has a content and a relational dimension: the content dimension involves the information being explicitly discussed, while the relational dimension expresses how you feel about the other person. Communication is irreversible, because it is impossible to "unreceive" a message; words and deeds, once said or done, are irretrievable. Communication is unrepeatable, because the same words and behavior are different each time they are spoken or performed.

3. What are four commonly held misconceptions about communication?

    Not all communication seeks understanding, as social rituals we enact every day attempt to influence others; deliberate ambiguity and deception are examples of communication in which understanding is not the primary goal. More communication is not always better, as excessive communication is unproductive or even aggravates a problem. Communication will not solve all problems, because even best-timed and best-planned communication cannot fix all problems. Effective communication is not a natural ability, because most people operate at a level of effectiveness far below their potential.

4. What are two ways that interpersonal communication can be defined?

    Interpersonal communication may be defined quantitatively or qualitatively. Quantitative definitions of interpersonal communication are based on the number of participants; when it is two it is called a dyad, so the terms "dyadic communication" and "interpersonal communication" may be used interchangeably since they are both interaction between two people. Qualitative definitions are based on the quality and nature of the interpersonal relationship, not the number of participants.

5. What is communication competence?

    It is defined as communication that is both effective and appropriate. The definition of what communication is appropriate in a given situation varies considerably from one culture to another. Competence is situational as communication competence is not absolute but exists in degrees or areas of competence. And competence can be learned.

Chapter 1: Answers to Thinking Outside the Box

1. Identify some of the nonverbal cues that are missing from computer-mediated communication (CMC), thus making the messages leaner.

   In particular, kinesics, haptics, and paralanguage are missing from CMC, making the messages much leaner. Body movement is missing from CMC interaction, which is called kinesics, which is the study of how people communicate through bodily movements. Touch is another type of nonverbal communication that is missing, and the study of touching is haptics. Paralanguage describes the way a message is spoken and vocal rate, pronunciation, pitch, tone volume and emphasis can change the meaning of words, and it is also missing.

2. Explain one of the forms that disinhibition can take in computer-mediated-communication (CMC) and the possible impact it might have on the relationship between communicators (Chapter 3).

   Disinhibition may lead to increased self-disclosure. There are benefits and risks of self-disclosure. Benefits of self-disclosure include catharsis, self-clarification, self-validation, reciprocity, impression formation, relationship maintenance and enhancement, moral obligation, social influence, and self-defense. Risks of self-disclosure include rejection, negative impression, decrease in relational satisfaction, loss of influence, loss of control, and hurt to the other person.

Chapter 2: Culture and Communication

SQ3R in Action

Generate an SQ3R chart for this chapter here:
http://www.teach-nology.com/web_tools/graphic_org/sq3r

Survey

Skim the title, key terms, chapter outline, objectives ("You should understand" and "You should be able to"), headings, tables, photos, cartoons, figures, charts, and items in the margin. Glance at the titles of the Focus on Research, Reflection, Film Clips, Self-Assessment, and Dark Side. At the end of each chapter, look over the Summary, Critical Thinking Probes, Ethical Challenges, Skill Builder, and Resources.

Question

Ask yourself questions. What do you know about these topics from your own life experiences and from other classes? Ask these six questions in each section: who, what, when, where, how, and why?

Read

Take one heading at a time and read to find the answers to the questions you've posed.

Recite

In your own words, say the answer aloud and then write it out.

Review

Review each section and then review the whole chapter. This is a good time to use the activities at the end of each chapter and the activities and the sample exams on the course website. Remember to periodically review the previous chapters as well.

Chapter 2: Outline

(Italicized words are key terms.)

I.   Fundamental concepts—Culture and intercultural communication
   A.   Culture and co-culture—*Culture* is a matter of perception and definition, and *co-culture* is a term used to describe the perception of membership in a group that is part of an encompassing culture.
      1.   *In-groups* are groups with which we identify.
      2.   *Out-groups* are groups that we view as different.
      3.   *Social identity* is the part of the self-concept that is based on membership in groups.

    B.   *Intercultural communication* describes the process that occurs when members of two or more cultures or co-cultures exchange messages in a manner that is influenced by their different cultural perceptions and symbol systems, both verbal and nonverbal.

    C.   To understand the relationship between interpersonal and intercultural communication, one model illustrates the relationship between interpersonal relationships and intercultural communication and shows that some interpersonal transactions have no cultural elements while others are almost exclusively intercultural and without personal dimensions.

    D.   Cultural differences are numerous, as there are a number of ways communication varies from one culture to another.

II.   Cultural values and norms are captured by five subtle yet vital values and norms that shape the way members of a culture communicate; these are as follows:

    A.   High- versus low-context—*Low-context culture* uses language primarily to express thoughts feelings and ideas as directly as possible, while *high-context culture* relies heavily on subtle, often nonverbal cues to maintain social harmony.

    B.   Individualism versus collectivism can be described as members of an *individualistic culture* viewing their primary responsibility as helping themselves, as opposed to members of a *collectivistic culture* feeling loyalties and obligations to their in-group.

    C.   *Power distance* describes the degree to which members of a society accept an unequal distribution of power.

    D.   *Uncertainty avoidance* is a term used to reflect the degree to which members of a culture feel threatened by ambiguous situations and how much they try to avoid them.

    E.   Achievement versus nurturing is described as *achievement culture* societies placing a high value on material success versus a *nurturing culture* regarding the support of relationships as an especially important goal.

III.   Codes relate to culture, as there are different verbal and nonverbal communication systems.

    A.   Verbal codes exist across cultures, as each language has its own unique style that distinguishes it from others; when a communicator tries to use the verbal style from one culture in a different one, problems are likely to arise.

    B.   Nonverbal codes exist; while there are similarities across codes, the range of differences in nonverbal behavior is tremendous.

    C.   When decoding messages, the potential for misunderstandings for communicators from different cultural backgrounds is great.

        1.   In translation, the potential for misunderstanding is always present.

        2.   Attribution is the process of making sense of another's behavior, and since most behavior is so ambiguous and may have several interpretations, the attribution process can lead to making faulty interpretations.

3. Patterns of thought vary in the way members of a culture are taught to think, and reason shapes they way they interpret others' messages.

IV. Developing intercultural communication competence involves having a set of skills and behaviors and being able to choose the appropriate one when needed.

A. Motivation and attitude describe the desire to communicate successfully with strangers, along with a cultural-general attitude.

B. Tolerance for ambiguity has to do with the level of uncertainty when encountering communicators from different cultures; intercultural communicators must welcome ambiguity.

C. Open-mindedness involves being free of *ethnocentrism,* which is an attitude that one's own culture is superior to others, and *prejudice*, which is an unfair and intolerant attitude toward others who belong to an out-group; *stereotyping* is applying prejudiced views about an entire group of people.

D. Knowledge and skill are needed for communicators to possess enough knowledge about other cultures to know how to best communicate, since communication with people from different backgrounds is culture-specific.

Chapter 2: Summary

Our world is increasingly connected by communication technology, so it is important to examine how communication works when members of different cultures interact. When people of different cultures interact, it presents another layer of challenges different from when members of the same culture communicate. Culture, as defined in the text, can be thought of as "the language, values, beliefs, traditions, and customs people share and learn." In-groups are groups with which we identify, and out-groups are groups which we view as different. Social identity is the part of the self-concept that is based on membership in groups. Co-culture describes the perception of membership in a group that is part of an encompassing culture.

Intercultural communication is the process that occurs when members of two or more cultures or co-cultures exchange messages in a manner that is influenced by their different cultural perceptions and symbol systems, both verbal and nonverbal. It is more accurate, however, to describe communication in degrees of cultural significance, since culture can play varying roles ranging from most to least intercultural. Not all interaction between different cultures is considered to be intercultural, since there must be a significant impact from cultural backgrounds, perceptions, and symbol systems of the participants. Salience is a term used to describe the value we attach to a particular person or phenomenon. There are cases where culture has little or no salience in relation to communication.

The relationship between intercultural communication and interpersonal relationships varies, ranging from interpersonal exchanges that have no intercultural elements, to exchanges that are purely intercultural and lacking interpersonal dimensions, to exchanges that contain elements of both.

There are a number of ways communication varies from one culture to another. In a low-context culture, language is used primarily to express thoughts, feelings, and ideas as directly as possible, which contrasts with a high-context culture, which relies heavily on subtle, often nonverbal cues to maintain social harmony. Individualistic cultures consider their primary responsibility to be to help themselves, while collectivistic cultures feel loyalties and obligations to an in-group. Power distance is the degree to which members of a society accept an unequal distribution of power. Uncertainty avoidance describes the degree to which members of a culture feel threatened by ambiguous situations and how much they try to avoid them. An achievement culture places high value on material success and tasks at hand, while a nurturing society regards the support of a relationship as an especially important goal.

There are important differences in the way people communicate with others of different cultures and with speakers of their own tongue. Each language has its own unique style that distinguishes it from others, and when a communicator tries to use the verbal style of a different culture, problems are bound to arise. Nonverbal codes range in differences between cultures as well. Decoding these messages, verbal and nonverbal, is a challenge. There can be challenges in translation, attributional variations, and patterns of thought.

In order to develop intercultural communication competence, one must possess the following traits: a tolerance for ambiguity, open-mindedness, knowledge, and skills. One should avoid ethnocentrism, which is an attitude that one's own culture is superior to others, and prejudice, which is an unfairly biased and intolerant attitude toward others who belong to an out-group.

Chapter 2: Key Terms

For each of these terms, define the term, give an example, and explain the significance of the term.

1. Achievement culture

2. Co-culture

3. Collectivistic culture

4. Culture

5. Ethnocentrism

6. High-context culture

7. Individualistic culture

48

8. In-group

9. Intercultural communication

10. Low-context culture

11. Nurturing culture

12. Out-group

13. Power distance

14. Prejudice

15. Salience

16. Social identity

17. Stereotyping

18. Uncertainty avoidance

Chapter 2: Review Questions

These questions are designed to help you better understand the concepts from this chapter and also allow you the opportunity to put the information into your own words. For practice true/false and multiple-choice questions, please refer to the course website.

1. What is the relationship between interpersonal communication and intercultural communication?

2. What are the five cultural values that shape the way members of a culture communicate?

3. Describe the five cultural values that shape the way members of a culture communicate.

4. When decoding messages, how can misunderstandings between communicators from different cultural backgrounds occur?

5. Identify and describe three skill sets needed to improve intercultural communication competence.

Chapter 2: Thinking Outside the Box: Synthesizing Your Knowledge

These questions are designed to help connect the course material from previous chapters.

1. Explain the relationship between communication competence (Chapter 1) and intercultural communication competence.

2. How can cognitive complexity (Chapter 1) aid in effective intercultural communication?

Chapter 2: Answers to Review Questions

1. What is the relationship between interpersonal communication and intercultural communication?

   The relationship between intercultural communication and interpersonal relationships varies, ranging from interpersonal exchanges that have no intercultural elements, to exchanges that are purely intercultural and lacking interpersonal dimensions, to exchanges that contain elements of both.

2. What are the five cultural values that shape the way members of a culture communicate?

   (1) High- versus low-context culture. (2) Individualism versus collectivism. (3) Power distance. (4) Uncertainty avoidance. (5) Achievement versus nurturing.

3. Describe the five cultural values that shape the way members of a culture communicate.

   (1) High- versus low-context—Low-context culture uses language primarily to express thoughts, feelings, and ideas as directly as possible, while high-context culture relies heavily on subtle, often nonverbal cues to maintain social harmony. (2) Individualism versus collectivism can be described as members of an individualistic culture viewing their primary responsibility as helping themselves, and members of collectivistic cultures feeling loyalties and obligations to their in-group. (3) Power distance describes the degree to which members of a society accept an unequal distribution of power. (4) Uncertainty avoidance is a term used to reflect the degree to which members of a culture feel threatened by ambiguous situations and how much they try to avoid them. (5) Achievement versus nurturing is described as achievement culture societies placing a high value on material success versus a nurturing culture regarding the support of relationships as an especially important goal.

4. When decoding messages, how can misunderstandings between communicators from different cultural backgrounds occur?

(1) In translation, the potential for misunderstanding is always present. (2) Attribution is the process of making sense of another's behavior, and since most behavior is ambiguous and may have several interpretations, the attribution process can lead to making faulty interpretations. (3) Patterns of thought vary in the way members of a culture are taught to think, and reason shapes they way they interpret others' messages.

5. Identify and describe three skill sets needed to improve intercultural communication competence.

(1) Motivation and attitude describe the desire to communicate successfully with strangers, along with a cultural-general attitude. (2) Tolerance for ambiguity is the level of uncertainty when encountering communicators from different cultures, and intercultural communicators must welcome ambiguity. (3) Open-mindedness involves being free of ethnocentrism, which is an attitude that one's own culture is superior to others, and prejudice, which is an unfair and intolerant attitude toward others who belong to an out-group; stereotyping is applying prejudiced views about an entire group of people.

Chapter 2: Answers to Thinking Outside the Box

1. Explain the relationship between communication competence (Chapter 1) and intercultural communication competence.

Communication competence includes the ability to be both effective and appropriate in one's communication, and there are many types of competent communication, including intercultural communication competence. Competence is situational and learned, but there are several common factors in effective communication; having a large repertoire of skills to choose the best one for the situation, adaptability to being able to choose the right message, and involvement with the other person make for more effective communication, as understanding another's point of view and having empathy offer the best chance at developing an effective message. More specifically, for intercultural communication competence, one must possess the following traits: a tolerance for ambiguity, open-mindedness, knowledge, and skills, while avoiding ethnocentrism, which is an attitude that one's own culture is superior to others.

2. How can cognitive complexity (Chapter 1) aid in effective intercultural communication?

Cognitive complexity is the ability to construct a variety of different frameworks for viewing an issue. Possessing a large number of constructs for interpreting the behavior of others increases the chances of acting in ways that will produce satisfying results. In intercultural communication situations, patterns of thought vary in the way members of a culture are taught to think, and reason shapes they way they interpret others' messages. Therefore, possessing cognitive complexity provides communicators with the ability to understand that individuals from another culture think about things differently, thus allowing more empathy to try to see things from other points of view.

Chapter 3: Communication and the Self

SQ3R in Action

Generate an SQ3R chart for this chapter here:
http://www.teach-nology.com/web_tools/graphic_org/sq3r

Survey

Skim the title, key terms, chapter outline, objectives ("You should understand" and "You should be able to"), headings, tables, photos, cartoons, figures, charts, and items in the margin. Glance at the titles of the Focus on Research, Reflection, Film Clips, Self-Assessment, and Dark Side. At the end of each chapter, look over the Summary, Critical Thinking Probes, Ethical Challenges, Skill Builder, and Resources.

Question

Ask yourself questions. What do you know about these topics from your own life experiences and from other classes? Ask these six questions in each section: who, what, when, where, how, and why?

Read

Take one heading at a time and read to find the answers to the questions you've posed.

Recite

In your own words, say the answer aloud and then write it out.

Review

Review each section and then review the whole chapter. This is a good time to use the activities at the end of each chapter and the activities and the sample exams on the course website. Remember to periodically review the previous chapters as well.

Chapter 3: Outline

(Italicized words are key terms.)

I. Communication affects *self-concept,* which is the relatively stable set of perceptions you hold for yourself, while *self-esteem* is the part of the self-concept that involves evaluations of self-worth.
   A. The self-concept develops as a rudimentary sense of self emerges at age six or seven months in humans and evolves through social interaction.
      1. *Reflected appraisal* is the process of mirroring the judgments of people surrounding one, while the term *significant other* is used to describe a person whose evaluations are especially influential.

2. *Social comparison* describes the way we evaluate ourselves in terms of how we compare with others and by comparing ourselves to *reference groups* or people we use to evaluate our own characteristics.

B. There are multiple characteristics of the self-concept.
  1. The self-concept is subjective, so that the way we view ourselves may not be the same way others view us.
  2. A healthy self-concept is flexible, so that it changes as needed to stay realistic.
  3. The self-concept resists change, as the tendency to resist revision of our self-concept is strong, and we seek out information that conforms to an existing self-concept, which is called *cognitive conservatism.*

C. The *self-fulfilling prophecy* occurs when a person's expectation of an event affects his or her behavior and therefore makes the predicted outcome more likely to occur than would have otherwise been true; the belief about the outcome affects communication.

D. Changing your self-concept is possible, and there are several methods for doing so.
  1. First, have realistic expectations, since some dissatisfaction may come from expecting too much from yourself.
  2. Second, have a realistic perception of yourself; one source of low self-esteem is inaccurate self-perception.

II. *Identity management* refers to the communication strategies people use to present the self and influence how others view them.

A. Each of us possesses several selves.
  1. The *perceived self* is the person each us believes we are when we examine ourselves.
  2. The *self* is the public image we present, which is normally a socially approved image.
  3. *Face* is the name given to the socially approved identity we present, and *facework* describes the verbal and nonverbal ways we act to maintain our face and the face of others.

B. There are multiple characteristics of identity management.
  1. We strive to construct multiple identities, as most people play a variety of roles in different areas of their lives, and being able to construct multiple identities is one element of competent communication.
  2. Identity management can be deliberate or unconscious; there are times when we are aware of managing impressions and times when we unconsciously act in ways that make an impression on others.
  3. People differ in the degree of identity management and range from extremely low self-monitoring to extremely high self-monitoring, but the ideal lies in flexibility.

C. We manage impressions in order to follow social rules and to achieve goals.

D. How we manage impressions is a question whose answer depends on the channel we choose.

          1.   Face-to-face identity management occurs by manner, appearance, and setting.

          2.   Identity management in mediated communication, and computer-mediated communication, offers an advantage to communicators who want to manage the impressions they make.

    E.   Identity management and honesty involves deciding which face to reveal depending upon the situation.

III.   Several factors distinguish self-disclosure from other types of communication, including: honesty, depth, availability of information, and context of sharing; furthermore, *self-disclosure* has the self as subject, is intentional, is directed at another person, is honest, is revealing, contains information generally unavailable from other sources, and gains much of its intimate nature from the context in which it is expressed.

    A.   There are two models of self-disclosure.

          1.   The *social penetration model* involves the breadth and depth of information involved.

          2.   The *Johari Window* is divided into information that one knows about oneself (known), things one doesn't know (unknown), things people know about one (blind), and things people don't know about one (hidden).

    B.   There are benefits and risks of self-disclosure; neither complete privacy nor complete disclosure is desirable.

          1.   Benefits of self-disclosure include catharsis, self-clarification, self-validation, reciprocity, impression formation, relationship maintenance and enhancement, moral obligation, social influence, and self-defense.

          2.   Risks of self-disclosure include rejection, negative impression, decrease in relational satisfaction, loss of influence, loss of control, and hurt to the other person.

    C.   There are alternatives to self-disclosure.

          1.   Silence is keeping information to yourself, and may be the best for you and the other person.

          2.   A *lie* is a deliberate attempt to hide or misrepresent the truth and is a sign of relational distress; however, a *benevolent lie* is not seen as malicious by the person who tells it, and the communicator thinks she or he is being helpful.

          3.   *Equivocal language* has two or more equally plausible meanings and is helpful in saving face in difficult situations.

          4.   Hinting is more direct than equivocal language.

          5.   There are ethics of evasion, as there are instances when hints, benevolent lies, and equivocations are ethical alternatives to self-disclosure.

    D.   There are some guidelines for self-disclosure.

          1.   Is the other person important to you? Disclosure may help develop a more personal relationship with someone.

          2.   Is the risk of disclosing reasonable? An analysis to determine if the benefits outweigh the risks may be helpful.

3.   Is the self-disclosure appropriate? Not all disclosure is appropriate at all times.
4.   Is the disclosure relevant to the situation at hand? Disclosure that is appropriate in highly personal relationships is not appropriate in less personal settings.
5.   Is the disclosure reciprocated? Unequal disclosure creates an unequal relationship.
6.   Will the effect be constructive? Self-disclosure must be used carefully, and the effect of the disclosure should be considered.

Chapter 3: Summary

Self-concept is the relatively stable set of perceptions you hold of yourself. Self-esteem is the part of the self-concept that involves evaluations of self-worth. The self-concept does not exist at birth; it develops as a product of social interaction. There are two theories that describe how interaction shapes the way individuals view themselves: reflected appraisal and social comparison. Reflected appraisal is the mirroring of the judgments of people around you. Social comparison is the process of evaluating ourselves in terms of how we compare with others. Reference groups are those people we use to evaluate our own characteristics. The self-concept has several characteristics: it is subjective, it is flexible, and it resists change. Cognitive conservatism is the tendency to seek information that conforms to an existing self-concept.

Self-fulfilling prophecy occurs when a person's expectations of an event, and her or his subsequent behavior based on those expectations, make the outcome more likely to occur than would otherwise have been true. There are two types of self-fulfilling prophecy, self-imposed prophecies occur when your own expectations influence your behavior, while the second category occurs when one person's expectations govern another's actions.

It is possible to change an unsatisfying self-concept. To do so, one should have realistic expectations, have a realistic perception of one's self, have the will to change, and have the skill to change by observing models.

Identity management is the set of communication strategies people use to influence how others view them. The perceived self is the person you believe yourself to be in moments of honest self-examination and is considered to be the "private self," because we don't reveal all of it to another person. The presenting self is a public image which is the way we want to appear to others. Face is the socially approved identity, and facework describes the verbal and nonverbal ways in which we act to maintain our own public image. There are some characteristics to identity management. We strive to construct multiple identities, and being able to do so is one element of communication competence. Identity management is collaborative, in that we improvise scenes where our character reacts with others. Identity management can be deliberate or unconscious, and people differ in their degrees of identity management.

People manage impressions in order to follow social rules and to accomplish personal goals. Creating a public face partially depends on which communication channel is chosen. Face-to-face identity management consists of three factors: manner, appearance, and setting. Identity management occurs in other types of communications, including mediated communication. Even though computer-mediated communication is unable to convey non-verbal cues, it can be an advantage, since communicators can more easily control the impressions they want to present to others. Self-disclosure is an important component of identity management and is characterized by honesty, depth, availability of information, and context of sharing. There are two models which help us understand self-disclosure. The social penetration model involves the breadth and depth of information volunteered. The Johari Window is a model that includes four parts: open, blind, hidden, and unknown, which refer to parts of a person that are unknown to either him/herself or to others.

There are benefits and risks of self-disclosure. The benefits include catharsis, self-clarification, self-validation, reciprocity, impression formation, relationship management and enhancement, moral obligation, social influence, and self-defense. The risks include rejection, negative impression, decrease in relational situation, loss of influence, loss of control, and it may hurt the other person.

There are alternatives to self-disclosure. These alternatives include silence, lying, equivocation, and hinting. A lie is a deliberate attempt to hide or misrepresent a truth and can be seen as a breach of ethics. A benevolent lie is a lie not seen by the teller as being malicious and is, instead, seen as being helpful. Equivocal language has two or more equally plausible meanings.

There are some guidelines for self-disclosure. The following questions should be asked in order to determine the correct level of self-disclosure. Is the other person important to you? Is the risk of disclosing reasonable? Is the self-disclosure appropriate? Is the disclosure relevant to the situation at hand? Is the disclosure reciprocated? Will the effect be constructive?

Chapter 3: Key Terms

For each of these terms, define the term, give an example, and explain the significance of the term.

1. Benevolent lie

2. Cognitive conservatism

3. Equivocal language

4. Face

5. Facework

6. Identity management

7. Johari Window

8. Lie

9. Perceived self

10. Presenting self

11. Reference groups

12. Reflected appraisal

13. Self-concept

14. Self-disclosure

15. Self-esteem

16. Self-fulfilling prophecy

17. Significant other

18. Social comparison

19. Social penetration model

Chapter 3: Review Questions

These questions are designed to help you better understand the concepts from this chapter and also allow you the opportunity to put the information into your own words. For practice true/false and multiple-choice questions, please refer to the course website.

1. Compare and contrast the concepts "reflected appraisal" and "social comparison."

2. What are the two models of self-disclosure?

3. What are some of the benefits and risks associated with self-disclosure?

4. Identify four alternatives to self-disclosure.

5. What are the six guidelines, or questions to ask, for self-disclosure?

Chapter 3: Thinking Outside the Box: Synthesizing Your Knowledge

These questions are designed to help connect the course material from previous chapters.

1. What is the relationship between the alternatives to self-disclosure and the assertion in Chapter 1 that not all communication seeks understanding (Chapter 1)?

2. What is the relationship between reflected appraisal, social comparison, and in-/out-group membership (Chapter 2)?

Chapter 3: Answers to Review Questions

1. Compare and contrast the concepts "reflected appraisal" and "social comparison."

   Reflected appraisal is the process of mirroring the judgments of surrounding people, whereas social comparison describes the way we evaluate ourselves in terms of how we compare with others and by comparing ourselves to reference groups or people we use to evaluate our own characteristics. In sum, reflected appraisal is the mirroring of the judgments of people around you, and social comparison is the process of evaluating ourselves in terms of how we compare with others.

2. What are the two models of self-disclosure?

   The social penetration model involves the breadth and depth of information involved. The Johari Window is a model that divides information that one knows about oneself (known), things one doesn't know (unknown), things people know about one (blind), and things people don't know about one (hidden).

3. What are some of the benefits and risks associated with self-disclosure?

   Benefits of self-disclosure include: catharsis, self-clarification, self-validation, reciprocity, impression formation, relationship maintenance and enhancement, moral obligation, social influence, and self-defense. Risks of self-disclosure include: rejection, negative impression, decrease in relational satisfaction, loss of influence, loss of control, and hurt to the other person.

4. Identify four alternatives to self-disclosure.

   (1) Silence is keeping information to yourself, and may be the best for you and the other person. (2) A lie is a deliberate attempt to hide or misrepresent the truth and is a sign of relational distress; however, a benevolent lie is not seen as malicious by the

person who tells it, and the communicator thinks she or he is being helpful. (3) Equivocal language has two or more equally plausible meanings and is helpful in saving face in difficult situations. (4) Hinting is more direct than equivocal language.

5. What are the six guidelines, or questions to ask, for self-disclosure?

    (1) Is the other person important to you? (2) Is the risk of disclosing reasonable? (3) Is the self-disclosure appropriate? (4) Is the disclosure relevant to the situation at hand? (5) Is the disclosure reciprocated? (6) Will the effect be constructive?

Chapter 3: Answers to Thinking Outside the Box

1. What is the relationship between the alternatives to self-disclosure and the assertion in Chapter 1 that not all communication seeks understanding (Chapter 1)?

    Not all communication seeks understanding. It is a flawed assumption that the goal of all communication is to maximize understanding between communicators; instead, social rituals we enact every day attempt to influence others. Deliberate ambiguity and deception are examples of communication in which understanding is not the primary goal. There are alternatives to self-disclosure, which help individuals manage face concerns. These alternatives include lying and equivocation. A benevolent lie is a lie not seen by the teller as being malicious and is, instead, seen as being helpful. Equivocal language has two or more equally plausible meanings.

2. What is the relationship between reflected appraisal, social comparison, and in-/out-group membership (Chapter 2)?

    Reflected appraisal is the mirroring of the judgments of people around you. Social comparison is the process of evaluating ourselves in terms of how we compare with others. In-groups are groups with which we identify. Out-groups are groups which we view as different. Social identity is the part of the self-concept that is based on membership in groups; therefore, those in our in-groups are going to have more impact on the processes of reflected appraisal and social comparison.

Chapter 4: Perceiving Others

SQ3R in Action

Generate an SQ3R chart for this chapter here:
        http://www.teach-nology.com/web_tools/graphic_org/sq3r

Survey

Skim the title, key terms, chapter outline, objectives ("You should understand" and "You should be able to"), headings, tables, photos, cartoons, figures, charts, and items in the margin. Glance at the titles of the Focus on Research, Reflection, Film Clips, Self-Assessment, and Dark Side. At the end of each chapter, look over the Summary, Critical Thinking Probes, Ethical Challenges, Skill Builder, and Resources.

Question

Ask yourself questions. What do you know about these topics from your own life experiences and from other classes? Ask these six questions in each section: who, what, when, where, how, and why?

Read

Take one heading at a time and read to find the answers to the questions you've posed.

Recite

In your own words, say the answer aloud and then write it out.

Review

Review each section and then review the whole chapter. This is a good time to use the activities at the end of each chapter and the activities and the sample exams on the course website. Remember to periodically review the previous chapters as well.

Chapter 4: Outline

(Italicized words are key terms.)

I.   The perception process refers to how our perceptions affect our communication with others.
        A.   Reality is constructed, as we create our reality with others through communication.
              1.   *First-order realities* are physically observable qualities of a thing or situation.
              2.   *Second-order realities* involve attaching meaning to first-order things or situations.

B. There are four steps in the perception process whereby we attach meanings to our experiences.
   1. *Selection* is the first step in perception, and stimuli that are intense often attract our attention.
   2. *Organization* is the stage where selected information must be arranged in some meaningful way in order to make sense of the world, and *punctuation* is a term used to describe the determination of causes and effects in a series of interactions.
   3. *Interpretation* plays a role in virtually every interpersonal act, since once we have selected and organized our perceptions; we interpret them in a way that makes sense.
   4. *Negotiation* is the process by which communicators influence each other's perceptions through communication, and one way to explain negotiation is to view interpersonal communication as the exchange of stories or *narratives* that we tell to describe our world.

II. How we select, organize, interpret, and negotiate information about others is influenced by a variety of factors.
   A. Physiological influences come from the physical environment and the ways that our bodies differ from others.
      1. Age allows for a greater scope and number of experiences, and developmental differences shape perceptions.
      2. Health and fatigue can have a strong impact on how you relate to others.
      3. Hunger can affect perception and communication.
      4. Biological cycles, including variations in body temperature, sexual drive, alertness, tolerance to stress, and mood, affect the way we relate to each other.
      5. Neurobehavioral challenges refer to differences in perception that are rooted in neurology, and such conditions as AD-HD and bipolar disorder influence perceptions.
   B. Psychological influences affect the way we perceive others.
      1. Our emotional state, or mood, strongly influences how we view people and events and therefore how we communicate.
      2. Our self-concept, or the way we think and feel about ourselves, strongly influences how we interpret others' behavior.
   C. Social influences are described in the *standpoint theory,* which states that a person's position in a society shapes her or his view of society in general and of specific individuals.
   D. Sex and gender roles theoretically describe how a person, regardless of his or her biological sex, can act in a masculine or feminine manner or exhibit both types of characteristics. These are referred to as *psychological sex types; androgynous* combines masculine and feminine traits, and *gender* is a shorthand term for psychological sex type.
   E. Our occupational role, or the kind of we work we do, also governs our view of the world.
   F. Cultural influences such as cultural selection, organization, interpretation, and negotiation exert a powerful influence on the way we view others' communication.

III.   *Attribution* describes the process of attaching meaning to behavior; there are several perceptual tendencies that may lead to inaccurate attributions.

    A.   We make snap judgments, which can become problematic when they are based on *stereotyping* or exaggerated beliefs associated with a categorizing system.

    B.   We cling to first impressions, because once we form an opinion of someone we tend to hang onto it and make any conflicting information fit our image.

        1.   The *halo effect* describes the tendency to form an overall positive impression of a person on the basis of one positive characteristic.

        2.   The *confirmation bias* is the term to describe the process of seeking out and organizing our impressions to support our initial opinion.

    C.   We judge ourselves more charitably than we do others, which is a tendency called *self-serving bias.*

    D.   We are influenced by our expectations, and this information is important when making decisions about others.

    E.   We are influenced by the obvious, which can be problematic when the most obvious factor is not necessarily the only cause.

    F.   We assume others are like us; we frequently mistakenly assume that others' views are similar to our own.

IV.   Since mismatched perceptions can interfere with communication, tools are needed to help others understand our perceptions and for us, in turn, to understand theirs.

    A.   *Perception checking* provides a good way to check and share interpretations.

    B.   *Empathy* is the ability to re-create another person's perspective, to experience the world from his or her point of view.

        1.   Empathy is valuable because the recipient of empathy receives self-esteem, a sense of comfort, and an ability to learn to trust the empathizer.

        2.   There is a link between empathy and ethical altruism.

        3.   The most important requirement for empathy is to be open-minded in order to understand another's position, but imagination and commitment are also needed.

Chapter 4: Summary

Our perceptions affect our communication, and we create our realities with others through communication. First-order realities are physically observable qualities of a thing or a situation. Second-order realities involve our attaching meaning to first-order things or situations.

We attach meanings to our experiences in four steps: selection, organization, interpretation, and negotiation. Selection is the first step of perception. Organization is when information is arranged in a meaningful way. Punctuation describes the determination of causes and effects in a series of interactions. Interpretation is influenced by several factors, including relational satisfaction, expectations, personal experience, and assumptions about human behavior.

Negotiation is the process by which communicators influence each other's perceptions. Interpersonal communication be seen as narratives, or stories used to describe our personal worlds.

There are several factors that influence perception. The physiological influences include the senses, age, health and fatigue, hunger, biological cycles, and neurobehavioral challenges. Psychological influences include mood and self-concept. Standpoint theory describes how a person's position in society shapes his or her view of society. Social influences include sex and gender roles as well as occupational roles.

Many factors distort the way we interpret the world. Attribution describes the process of attaching meaning to behavior. People attribute meaning to both their actions and the actions of others; but we judge our own behavior differently than that of others. We judge ourselves more charitably than we do others, which is self-serving bias. There are several tendencies that may lead to inaccurate attributions. We make snap judgments which can be problematic if they are based on stereotyping, which is exaggerated beliefs associated with a categorizing system. We cling to first impressions. The halo effect is the tendency to form an overall positive impression of a person on the basis of one positive characteristic. Confirmation bias describes the process of seeking out and organizing our impressions to support our first opinion. We are influenced by our expectations and by what seems obvious, and we tend to assume others are similar to us.

Perception checking provides an effective way to check and share interpretations. Building empathy, or the ability to re-create another person's perspective, is crucial to understanding other people. Empathy provides increased self-esteem and comfort to the recipient and is linked to being an ethical person. In order to be empathic, one must be open-minded, possess imagination, and be committed.

Chapter 4: Key Terms

For each of these terms, define the term, give an example, and explain the significance of the term.

1. Androgynous

2. Attribution

3. Confirmation bias

4. Empathy

5. First-order realities

6. Gender

7. Halo effect

8. Interpretation

9. Narrative

10. Negotiation

11. Organization

12. Perception checking

13. Psychological sex type

14. Punctuation

15. Second-order realities

16. Selection

17. Self-serving bias

18. Standpoint theory

19. Stereotyping

Chapter 4: Review Questions

These questions are designed to help you better understand the concepts from this chapter and also allow you the opportunity to put the information into your own words. For practice true/false and multiple-choice questions, please refer to the course website.

1. Describe the four steps of the perception process.

2. Identify the factors that influence perception.

3. Describe the different gender roles and how they affect perception.

4. Explain why we tend to cling to first impressions.

5. Define empathy and explain its importance to perception.

Chapter 4: Thinking Outside the Box: Synthesizing Your Knowledge

These questions are designed to help connect the course material from previous chapters.

1. Explain the relationship between gender and culture (Chapter 2) as it relates to intercultural communication (Chapter 2).

2. What is the relationship between cognitive complexity (Chapter 1) and empathy?

Chapter 4: Answers to Review Questions

1. Describe the four steps of the perception process.

   Selection is the first step in perception, and stimuli that are intense often attract our attention. Organization is the stage where selected information must be arranged in some meaningful way in order to make sense of the world, and punctuation is a term used to describe the determination of causes and effects in a series of interactions. Next, interpretation plays a role in virtually every interpersonal act, since once we have selected and organized our perceptions we interpret them in a way that makes sense. Last, negotiation is the process by which communicators influence each other's perceptions through communication.

2. Identify the factors that influence perception.

   Physiological influences include the senses, age, health and fatigue, hunger, biological cycles, and neurobehavioral challenges. Psychological influences include mood and self-concept. Standpoint theory describes how a person's position in society shapes his or her view of society. Social influences include sex and gender roles as well as occupational roles.

3. Describe the different gender roles and how they affect perception.

   Gender roles are not defined by biological sex. Gender roles address how individuals may behave in a masculine or feminine manner. Individuals who exhibit both types of characteristics are referred to as androgynous.

4. Explain why we tend to cling to first impressions.

   The halo effect describes the tendency to form an overall positive impression of a person on the basis of one positive characteristic. Confirmation bias is the term used to describe the process of seeking out and organizing our impressions to support our initial impression.

5. Define empathy and explain its importance to perception.

Building empathy, or the ability to re-create another person's perspective, is crucial to understanding other people. Empathy provides increased self-esteem and comfort to the recipient and is linked to being an ethical person. In order to be empathic, one must be open-minded, possess imagination, and be committed.

Chapter 4: Answers to Thinking Outside the Box

1. Explain the relationship between gender and culture (Chapter 2) as it relates to intercultural communication (Chapter 2).

Intercultural communication describes the process that occurs when members of two or more cultures or co-cultures exchange messages in a manner that is influenced by their different cultural perceptions and symbol systems, both verbal and nonverbal. Males and females have different cultural perceptions, symbolic systems, and varying ways of verbally and nonverbally communicating. Sex and gender roles theoretically describe how a person, regardless of his or her biological sex, can act in a masculine or feminine manner or exhibit both types of characteristics, which is referred to as being androgynous. In sum, gender roles define different cultural groups.

2. What is the relationship between cognitive complexity (Chapter 1) and empathy?

Cognitive complexity is the ability to construct a variety of different frameworks for viewing an issue. Possessing a large number of constructs for interpreting the behavior of others increases the chances of acting in ways that will produce satisfying results. Empathy is the ability to re-create another person's perspective, to experience the world from his or her point of view, and is valuable because the recipient of empathy receives self-esteem, a sense of comfort, and an ability to learn to trust the empathizer. The most important aspect of being empathic is to be open minded, which requires cognitive complexity, in order to understand another's position; but imagination and commitment are also needed.

Chapter 5: Language

SQ3R in Action

Generate an SQ3R chart for this chapter here:
http://www.teach-nology.com/web_tools/graphic_org/sq3r

Survey

Skim the title, key terms, chapter outline, objectives ("You should understand" and "You should be able to"), headings, tables, photos, cartoons, figures, charts, and items in the margin. Glance at the titles of the Focus on Research, Reflection, Film Clips, Self-Assessment, and Dark Side. At the end of each chapter, look over the Summary, Critical Thinking Probes, Ethical Challenges, Skill Builder, and Resources.

Question

Ask yourself questions. What do you know about these topics from your own life experiences and from other classes? Ask these six questions in each section: who, what, when, where, how, and why?

Read

Take one heading at a time and read to find the answers to the questions you've posed.

Recite

In your own words, say the answer aloud and then write it out.

Review

Review each section and then review the whole chapter. This is a good time to use the activities at the end of each chapter and the activities and the sample exams on the course website. Remember to periodically review the previous chapters as well.

Chapter 5: Outline

(Italicized words are key terms.)

I.   The nature of language is characterized by the following features.
  A.   Language is symbolic; words are symbols and have no inherent meanings.
  B.   Language is rule-governed, as is illustrated by the following rules.
    1.   *Phonological rules* govern how sounds are combined to form words.
    2.   *Syntactic rules* govern the way symbols can be arranged.
    3.   *Semantic rules* help us understand the meaning of individual words.

4. *Pragmatic rules* tell us what uses and interpretations of a message are appropriate in a given context.

C. Language is subjective; people attach different meanings to the same message.

D. Language and worldview can be understood by the theory *linguistic relativism*, which states that a culture is shaped and reflected by the language its members speak. The best known declaration of linguistic relativism is the *Sapir–Whorf hypothesis,* which states that concepts do not exist if the words for them do not exist.

II. Language can have a strong effect on our perceptions and how we regard one another.

A. Names are a reflection of ethnic identity and an indicator of status.

B. Speech can also be a way of building and demonstrating solidarity with others, known as "affiliation."

1. *Convergence* is the process of adapting one's speech style to match that of others with whom the communicator wants to identify.

2. *Divergence* is the strategy of speaking in a way that emphasizes differences between communicators and others.

C. There are a number of language patterns that add to or detract from a speaker's *power* to influence others.

D. Sexism and racism can affect the self-concepts of women and men.

1. *Sexist language* uses words, phrases, and expressions that unnecessarily differentiate between female and male.

2. *Racist language* reflects a worldview that classifies members of one racial group as superior and others as inferior.

III. Language can shape the way we perceive and understand the world, but potential problems can arise out of language as well.

A. The goal of language is not always clarity, and vagueness serves useful purposes.

1. *Ambiguous language* consists of words and phrases that have more than one commonly accepted definition, which can cause problems and can also be useful at the same time.

2. Abstraction can be used at a high level to generalize about similarities between several objects, people, ideas, or events and can be thought of as being on an *abstraction ladder.*

3. A *euphemism* is an innocuous term substituted for a blunt one and is typically used to soften the impact of information that might be unpleasant.

4. *Relative language* gains meaning by comparison and is vague because the relative word is not linked to a more measurable term.

5. *Static evaluation* is a description or evaluation that contains the word "is," which makes the mistaken assumption that people or things are consistent and unchanging.

B. Language reflects the speaker's willingness to take responsibility for his or her beliefs, feelings, and actions.

1. *"It" statements* replace the personal pronoun "I" with "it," which avoids responsibility for ownership of a message.

2. A *"but" statement* has the effect of canceling the thought that precedes it.

3. *"I" language* is a way of accepting responsibility, while *"You" language* expresses judgment of another person, and *"We" language* implies joint concern and responsibility for both the speaker and receiver.

4. Fact-opinion confusion occurs when *factual statements* are claims that can be verified as true or false, while *opinion statements* are based on the speaker's beliefs and can never be proven or disproven.

5. Fact-inference confusion may occur when *inferential statements* are conclusions arrived at from interpretation of events; arguments often arise when we label our inferences as facts.

6. *Emotive language* seems to describe something but in reality announces the speaker's attitude toward it.

IV. There are similarities and differences in the way females and males use language.

   A. There are three approaches that represent three different sides in the gender and language debate.

      1. "Fundamental differences" have been identified by social scientists who have acknowledged that there are some fundamental differences in the way men and women behave socially; some take this theory to mean that men and women grow up with different rules about how to act and speak.

      2. "Important differences" describe the stance of most communication scholars, who acknowledge that are some significant differences in the way women and men use language.

      3. "Minor differences" are believed in by some communication scholars, who point to research that shows that when differences exist, they are often small and are matters of degree and not kind.

   B. When accounting for gender differences, occupation, gender role, and power trump sex differences.

Chapter 5: Summary

Some features characterize all languages, and these features explain both why language is such a useful tool and why it can cause challenges. Language is symbolic, as words have no meanings in and of themselves. Language is rule-governed. Phonological rules govern how sounds are combined to form words, while syntactic rules govern the ways symbols can be arranged. Semantic rules govern the meanings of statements. Pragmatic rules help us to distinguish the accurate meanings of speech by telling us what uses and interpretations of a message are appropriate in a given context. Language is subjective.

Linguistic relativism is the theory that the worldview of a culture is shaped and reflected by the language its members speak. The Sapir–Whorf hypothesis is the best known declaration of linguistic relativism and theorizes that cultures cannot comprehend concepts if they do not have words for those concepts.

Speech can be a way of building and demonstrating solidarity with others. Convergence is the act of adapting one's speech style to match that of others with whom the communicator wants to identify. Divergence is speaking in a way that emphasizes differences between the speaker and receiver(s).

Language patterns add to or detract from a speaker's power to influence others. Sexist language includes words, phrases, and expression that "unnecessarily differentiate between females and males or exclude, trivialize, or diminish" either sex; it affects the self-concepts of both women and men. There are two methods to eliminate sexist language. The first is to substitute neutral terms for sex-specific terms, while the second method takes a different approach and marks sex clearly in communication. Racist language reflects a worldview that classifies members of one racial group as superior and others as inferior.

Language can be used to make ideas clear to people or to make ourselves less than clear. Ambiguous language consists of words and phrases that have more than one commonly accepted definition. High-level abstractions are ways to generalize similarities between several objects, people, ideas, or events. An abstraction ladder is a way of ordering abstractions by hierarchy. Euphemisms are neutral terms substituted for blunt ones. Relative language gains meaning by comparison. Static evaluation is a description of a person or thing that contains the word "is" and mistakenly assumes that people or things are consistent and immutable.

"It" statements replace the personal pronoun "I" with the more impersonal "it." "I" language clearly identifies the speaker as the source of the message. "But" statements are confusing, since they cancel the thought that precedes them. "You" language expresses judgment of the other person. "We" language implies that the issue is a concern and responsibility of both the speaker and the receiver of the message.

Factual statements are claims that can be verified as true or false. Opinion statements are based on the speaker's beliefs. Inferential statements are conclusions arrived at from an interpretation of evidence and can cause relational difficulties. Emotive language seems to describe something but really announces the speaker's attitude toward it.

There are three approaches that represent three different sides in the gender and language debate. The first approach, called fundamental differences, argues that men and women are fundamentally different and can be described as being members of distinct cultures. The second approach is important differences, which describes a theory in which scholars acknowledge that there are some significant differences in the way men and women use language. The third approach is the minor differences approach, which states that the link between sex and language use isn't clear-cut. Occupation can trump gender as an influence on speaking style, while each person's gender role is another power force that influences his or her speech style.

Chapter 5: Key Terms

For each of these terms, define the term, give an example, and explain the significance of the term.

1. Abstraction ladder

2. Ambiguous language

3. "But" statement

4. Convergence

5. Divergence

6. Emotive language

7. Euphemism

8. Factual statement

9. "I" language

10. Inferential statement

11. "It" statement

12. Linguistic relativism

13. Opinion statement

14. Phonological rules

15. Powerless speech mannerisms

16. Pragmatic rules

17. Racist language

18. Relative language

19. Sapir–Whorf hypothesis

20. Semantic rules

21. Sexist language

22. Static evaluation

23. Syntactic rules

24. "We" language

25. "You" language

Chapter 5: Review Questions

These questions are designed to help you better understand the concepts from this chapter and also allow you the opportunity to put the information into your own words. For practice true/false and multiple-choice questions, please refer to the course website.

1. Identify and define the three rules that govern language.

2. Explain the Sapir–Whorf hypothesis.

3. Explain how speech can be a way of building and demonstrating solidarity with others.

4. Explain how language reflects the speaker's willingness to take responsibility for his or her beliefs, feelings, and actions.

5. What are the three approaches that represent the different sides of the gender and language debate?

Chapter 5: Thinking Outside the Box: Synthesizing Your Knowledge

These questions are designed to help connect the course material from previous chapters.

1. What is the relationship between language adaptation and perceived group membership (Chapter 2)?

2. What is the relationship between lying (Chapter 3) and the different types of unclear language?

Chapter 5: Answers to Review Questions

1. Identify and define the three rules that govern language.

   Phonological rules govern how sounds are combined to form words, while syntactic rules govern the ways symbols can be arranged. Semantic rules govern the meanings of statements. Pragmatic rules help us to distinguish the accurate meanings of speech by telling us what uses and interpretations of a message are appropriate in a given context.

2. Explain the Sapir–Whorf hypothesis.

   It describes linguistic relativism by theorizing that cultures cannot comprehend concepts if they do not have words for those concepts.

3. Explain how speech can be a way of building and demonstrating solidarity with others.

   Affiliation describes how individuals demonstrate solidarity with one another. This may occur through convergence, which is the process of adapting one's speech style to match that of others with whom the communicator wants to identify; rather than divergence, which is the strategy of speaking in a way that emphasizes differences between communicators and others.

4. Explain how language reflects the speaker's willingness to take responsibility for his or her beliefs, feelings, and actions.

   It-I-You-We language: "It" statements replace the personal pronoun "I" with "it," which avoids responsibility for ownership of a message. "But" statements have the effect of canceling the thought that precedes them. "I" language is a way of accepting responsibility, while "You" language expresses judgment of another person, and "We" language implies joint concern and responsibility for both the speaker and the receiver.

Fact-opinion confusion occurs when factual statements are claims that can be verified as true or false, while opinion statements are based on the speaker's beliefs and can never be proven or disproven. Fact-inference confusion may occur when inferential statements are conclusions arrived at from interpretation of events, and arguments often arise when we label our inferences as facts. Emotive language seems to describe something, but in reality announces the speaker's attitude toward it.

5. What are the three approaches that represent the different sides of the gender and language debate?

    The first approach, called fundamental differences, argues that men and women are fundamentally different and can be described as being members of distinct cultures. The second approach is important differences, which describes a theory in which scholars acknowledge that there are some significant differences in the way men and women use language. The third approach is the minor differences approach, which states that the link between sex and language use is not clear-cut.

Chapter 5: Answers to Thinking Outside the Box

1. What is the relationship between language adaptation and perceived group membership (Chapter 2)?

    Convergence is the process of adapting one's speech style to match that of others with whom the communicator wants to identify. In-groups are groups with which we identify. Divergence is the strategy of speaking in a way that emphasizes differences between communicators and others. Out-groups are groups that we view as different.

2. What is the relationship between lying (Chapter 3) and the different types of unclear language?

    A lie is a deliberate attempt to hide or misrepresent a truth and can be seen is a breach of ethics. A benevolent lie is a lie not seen by the teller as being malicious and is, instead, seen as being helpful. The goal of language is not always clarity, and vagueness serves useful purposes, as a means of benevolent lying. Ambiguous language consists of words and phrases that have more than one commonly accepted definition; it can cause problems and is also useful at the same time. Abstraction can be used at a high level to generalize about similarities between several objects, people, ideas, or events and can be thought of as being on an abstraction ladder. A euphemism is an innocuous term substituted for blunt one and is typically used to soften the impact of information that might be unpleasant. Relative language gains meaning by comparison and is vague because the relative word was not linked to a more measurable term.

Chapter 6: Nonverbal Communication

SQ3R in Action

Generate an SQ3R chart for this chapter here:
http://www.teach-nology.com/web_tools/graphic_org/sq3r

Survey

Skim the title, key terms, chapter outline, objectives ("You should understand" and "You should be able to"), headings, tables, photos, cartoons, figures, charts, and items in the margin. Glance at the titles of the Focus on Research, Reflection, Film Clips, Self-Assessment, and Dark Side. At the end of each chapter, look over the Summary, Critical Thinking Probes, Ethical Challenges, Skill Builder, and Resources.

Question

Ask yourself questions. What do you know about these topics from your own life experiences and from other classes? Ask these six questions in each section: who, what, when, where, how, and why?

Read

Take one heading at a time and read to find the answers to the questions you've posed.

Recite

In your own words, say the answer aloud and then write it out.

Review

Review each section and then review the whole chapter. This is a good time to use the activities at the end of each chapter and the activities and the sample exams on the course website. Remember to periodically review the previous chapters as well.

Chapter 6: Outline

(Italicized words are key terms.)

I.   *Nonverbal Communication* describes the messages expressed by nonlinguistic means.

II.   Characteristics of Nonverbal Communication include the following:

    A.   Nonverbal communication is influenced by culture; *emblems* are culturally understood substitutes for verbal expressions.

    B.   Nonverbal communication is primarily relational, in that it allows us to define the kind of relationships we want to have with others as well as allowing us to convey emotions that we are either unable or unwilling to express vocally.

C.   Nonverbal communication is ambiguous, since an action can be interpreted many different ways.

III.   Nonverbal cues play important roles in how we relate to others.

    A.   Creating and maintaining relationships is a function of nonverbal communication, since we observe nonverbal cues in the early stages of a relationship, and nonverbal cues provide a clear sign of relational satisfaction.

    B.   *Regulators* are cues that help control verbal interaction, such as the turn-taking signals in conversation.

    C.   We use nonverbal behavior in ways that get others to satisfy our wants and desires; examples of nonverbal behavior are: looking directly at someone, wearing high-status clothes, and using touch.

    D.   The messages we send and receive are not always truthful, and people can learn the nonverbal cues of lying, which may include stammering, hesitation, and increased vocal pitch.

    E.   Managing identity is getting others to see us as we want to be seen; there are several ways of managing identity nonverbally.

        1.   "Manner" refers to the way we act.

        2.   "Appearance" involves the way we dress, artifacts we wear, etc.

        3.   "Setting" involves the physical items we surround ourselves with.

IV.   Types of Nonverbal Communication

    A.   Face and eyes are the most noticeable part of the body; the study of how eyes communicate is known as *oculesics*.

    A.   Body movement is another type of nonverbal communication.

        1.   *Kinesics* describes the study of how people communicate through body movements.

        2.   *Manipulators* are what social scientists call gestures that consist of fidgeting, or one part of the body manipulating another.

    C.   Touch plays a large part in how we respond to others; *haptics* is the term used to describe the study of touching.

    D.   Voice-emphasis and tone of voice can change the meaning of a message.

        1.   *Paralanguage* describes the way a message is spoken; vocal rate, pronunciation, pitch, tone, volume, and emphasis can give the same word or words many meanings.

        2.   *Disinfluencies* include stammering and are a type of paralanguage.

    E.   We have preferred distances when dealing with people.

        1.   *Proxemics* is the study of how communication is affected by the use, organization, and perception of space and distance.

        2.   *Personal space* refers to the invisible bubble that puts distance between ourselves and others.

        3.   *Intimate distance* is skin contact to about 18 inches and is reserved for people who are emotionally close to us and in mostly private situations.

        4.   *Personal distance* ranges from 18 inches to 4 feet.

        5.   *Social distance* ranges from about 4 feet to 12 feet.

        6.   *Public distance* runs outward from 12 feet.

    F.   *Territory* is stationary personal space, such as choosing a seat at the corner of an empty table.

G.   The way we handle time can express both intentional and unintentional messages; *chronemics* is the study of how humans use and structure time.

H.   Physical Attractiveness affects social interaction between people and is a perception that can be enhanced through good communication skills.

I.   Clothing is a means of nonverbal communication and can convey at least 10 messages to others, such as economic and educational level.

J.   Physical environment can communicate information and also shape the kind of interaction that occurs.

Chapter 6: Summary

Nonverbal communication refers to messages expressed by nonlinguistic means. What we do often conveys more meaning than what we say, as 93 percent of the emotional impact of a message comes from a nonverbal source.

There are many types of nonverbal communication, such as gestures, facial expressions, and posture, but all types share some characteristics. All behavior has communicative value, as it is impossible not to communicate. Nonverbal communication is primarily relational in that it allows us to define the kind of relationships we want to have with others. Nonverbal communication is ambiguous, since there are many different meanings that can be attributed to nonverbal cues. Nonverbal communication is influenced by culture. Emblems are culturally understood substitutes for verbal expressions.

There are many functions of nonverbal communication, including creating and maintaining relationships. In the beginning of relationships we observe nonverbal cues while providing nonverbal cues about ourselves. In established relationships, nonverbal cues offer a clear sign of relational satisfaction. Nonverbal regulators are cues which function to help control verbal interaction, while another function of nonverbal communication is to influence others. Nonverbal cues can be used also to help receivers realize that the speaker is trying to conceal or deceive and can be more important than verbal messages in creating impressions.

There are many types of nonverbal communication. The nonverbal messages from the face and eyes are very difficult to read. Oculesics is the study of how eyes communicate. Body movement is another way of communicating nonverbally, and kinesics is the study of how people communicate through bodily movements. Fidgeting is a group of ambiguous gestures and includes movement where one body part manipulates another. These behaviors are called manipulators. Touch is another type of nonverbal communication, and the study of touching is haptics. Touch plays a large part in how we respond to each other, increasing liking and boosting compliance.

Paralanguage describes the way a message is spoken; vocal rate, pronunciation, pitch, tone, volume, and emphasis can change the meaning of words. Paralanguage also includes length of pauses and disinfluences such as stammering or use of such filler words as "er." Listeners pay more attention to paralanguage than to the content of words when asked to determine a speaker's attitude.

Proximity is the study of how communication is affected by the use, organization, and perception of space and distance. Each of us has an understanding of personal space, and the distance we put between ourselves and others gives a nonverbal clue to our feelings. Intimate distance is the space we use with people who are emotionally close to us, which begins with skin contact and goes to about 18 inches away from us; personal distance ranges from 18 inches to 4 feet; social distance is 4 to 12 feet; and public distance runs outward from 12 feet. Territory is the space which serves as an extension of our physical being and remains stationary.

Chronemics is the study of how humans use and structure time, and the way we handle time can express intentional and unintentional messages. Physical attractiveness affects how people are treated. Clothing is a means of nonverbal communication by conveying messages of economic level, education level, trustworthiness, social position, level of sophistication, economic background, social background, educational background, level of success, and moral character.

Physical environment provides and affects communication at the same time. An environment can communicate information about the designer or the inhabitant while at the same time it can shape the interaction that takes place in it.

Chapter 6: Key Terms

For each of these terms, define the term, give an example, and explain the significance of the term.

1. Chronemics

2. Disfluencies

3. Emblems

4. Haptics

5. Intimate distance

6. Kinesics

7. Manipulators

8. Nonverbal communication

9. Oculesics

10. Paralanguage

11. Personal distance

12. Personal space

13. Proxemics

14. Public distance

15. Regulators

16. Social distance

17. Territory

Chapter 6: Review Questions

These questions are designed to help you better understand the concepts from this chapter and also allow you the opportunity to put the information into your own words. For practice true/false and multiple-choice questions, please refer to the course website.

1. What are the three characteristics of nonverbal communication?

2. Identify and explain the three ways of managing identity nonverbally.

3. Identify and describe the types of nonverbal communication.

4. What nonverbal cues are useful for detecting lying?

5. According to the study of proxemics, what are the preferred distances, or personal spaces, when dealing with people?

Chapter 6: Thinking Outside the Box: Synthesizing Your Knowledge

These questions are designed to help connect the course material from previous chapters.

1. What is the role of nonverbal communication in the statement, "every message has both a content and relational dimension," as explained in the first chapter (Chapter 1)?

2. How might culture (Chapter 2) shape the nonverbal dimension of the physical environment?

Chapter 6: Answers to Review Questions

1. What are the three characteristics of nonverbal communication?

   (1) Nonverbal communication is influenced by culture, and emblems are culturally understood substitutes for verbal expressions. (2) Nonverbal communication is primarily relational in that it allows us to define the kind of relationships we want to have with others as well as allowing us to convey emotions that we are either unable or unwilling to express vocally. (3) Nonverbal communication is ambiguous, since an action can be interpreted many different ways.

2. Identify and explain the three ways of managing identity nonverbally.

   (1) Manner refers to the way we act. (2) Appearance involves the way we dress, artifacts we wear, etc. (3) Setting involves the physical items we surround ourselves with.

3. Identify and describe the types of nonverbal communication.

   Face and eyes are the most noticeable part of the body; the study of how eyes communicate is known as oculesics. Kinesics describes the study of how people communicate through body movements. Touch plays a large part in how we respond to others, and haptics is the term used to describe the study of touching. Paralanguage describes the way a message is spoken; vocal rate, pronunciation, pitch, tone, volume, and emphasis can give the same word or words many meanings. Proxemics is the study of how communication is affected by the use, organization, and perception of space and distance. The way we handle time can express both intentional and unintentional messages, and chronemics is the study of how humans use and structure time. Physical Attractiveness affects social interaction between people and is a perception that can be enhanced through good communication skills. Physical Environment can communicate information and also shape the kind of interaction that occurs.

4. What nonverbal cues are useful for detecting lying?

   Stammering, hesitation, and increased vocal pitch are nonverbal indicators of lying.

5. According to the study of proxemics, what are the preferred distances, or personal spaces, when dealing with people?

   Intimate distance ranges from skin contact to about 18 inches and is reserved for people who are emotionally close to us and in mostly private situations. Personal distance ranges from 18 inches to 4 feet away. Social distance ranges from about 4 feet to 12 feet out. Public distance runs outward from 12 feet.

Chapter 6: Answers to Thinking Outside the Box

1. What is the role of nonverbal communication in the statement, "every message has both a content and relational dimension," as explained in the first chapter (Chapter 1)?

   Messages are both content-oriented and relational, meaning that information is not the only thing exchanged in messages. Often, how the speaker feels about the recipient is also expressed, which is the relational-level meaning. Relational messages are expressed primarily through nonverbal channels, such as paralanguage, or how the speaker talks.

2. How might culture (Chapter 2) shape the nonverbal dimension of the physical environment?

   Physical environment is communicative, and it affects communication at the same time. An environment can communicate information about the designer or the inhabitant while at the same time it can shape the interaction that takes place in it. Individuals who design physical environments are likely to include cultural artifacts, which reflect one's cultural experience.

Chapter 7: Listening: Understanding and Supporting Others

SQ3R in Action

Generate an SQ3R chart for this chapter here:
http://www.teach-nology.com/web_tools/graphic_org/sq3r

Survey

Skim the title, key terms, chapter outline, objectives ("You should understand" and "You should be able to"), headings, tables, photos, cartoons, figures, charts, and items in the margin. Glance at the titles of the Focus on Research, Reflection, Film Clips, Self-Assessment, and Dark Side. At the end of each chapter, look over the Summary, Critical Thinking Probes, Ethical Challenges, Skill Builder, and Resources.

Question

Ask yourself questions. What do you know about these topics from your own life experiences and from other classes? Ask these six questions in each section: who, what, when, where, how, and why?

Read

Take one heading at a time and read to find the answers to the questions you've posed.

Recite

In your own words, say the answer aloud and then write it out.

Review

Review each section and then review the whole chapter. This is a good time to use the activities at the end of each chapter and the activities and the sample exams on the course website. Remember to periodically review the previous chapters as well.

Chapter 7: Outline

(Italicized words are key terms.)

I.   The nature of listening is complex.
    A.   Listening is the most frequent and important form of communication and is often considered a more valued skill than speaking.
    B.   *Listening* is the process of making sense of others' spoken messages, while hearing is the physical process of receiving the message and is automatic, unlike listening.
        1.   *Mindless listening* occurs when we react automatically and routinely, without mental investment, to messages.

        2.   *Mindful listening* is when careful and thoughtful attention is paid to messages received.

  C.   Reasons for listening vary, and each reason requires a different set of attitudes and skills.

        1.   To understand, as the most obvious reason is to understand and retain information. *Listening fidelity* is a term used to describe the degree of congruence between what a listener understands and what the message-sender was attempting to communicate.

        2.   To evaluate means to judge the quality of the message.

        3.   To build and maintain relationships; this occurs through effective listening, as it helps builds better relationships, according to research.

        4.   To help others, because when people listen to others with understanding and concern, they can gain different and useful perspectives for solving problems.

II.   Listening is a challenge, as there are obstacles to overcome when listening carefully is the objective.

  A.   Listening is not easy, and there are several barriers to listening.

        1.   Information overload is a result of a barrage of messages; people often choose to listen mindlessly instead of mindfully.

        2.   Personal concerns can hinder listening; people are often distracted by matters of more immediate concern than the messages others are sending.

        3.   Rapid thought can get in the way of careful listening, because our minds are active; the brain works faster than a person can speak.

        4.   Noise presents both physical and psychological distractions.

  B.   All listeners do not receive the same message; since people bring personal perspectives and experiences into every interaction, people can never completely understand each other.

  C.   Poor listening habits exist; most people possess one or more bad habits that keep them from understanding others' messages.

        1.   *Pseudolistening* is an imitation of actual listening.

        2.   *Stage hogging* is when listeners are interested only in expressing their ideas and don't care about what anyone else has to say.

        3.   *Selective listening* is when listeners respond only to the parts of a message that interest them.

        4.   *Filling in gaps* is what people do when they like to think that they remember a whole story and manufacture information to complete the picture.

        5.   *Insulated listening* is when someone fails to hear or acknowledge something in a message.

        6.   *Defensive listening* is when someone takes innocent comments as personal attacks.

        7.   *Ambushing* is listening carefully but only to gather information to later use against the speaker.

III.   Listening consists of five elements.

  A.   *Hearing* is the physiological aspect of listening.

      B.   *Attending* is the psychological process of listening and is part of the process of selection.

      C.   *Understanding* is composed of several elements: awareness of the rules of the language, knowledge of the source of the message, and mental ability.

      D.   *Remembering* is the ability to recall information.

      E.   *Responding* is the final step of the listening process and involves offering feedback to the speaker.

IV.   There are eight types of listening responses.

      A.   *Silent listening* is staying attentive and responsive nonverbally.

      B.   *Questioning* occurs when the listener asks the speaker for additional information.

           1.   *Open questions* allow for extended responses.

           2.   *Closed questions* allow only a limited range of answers.

           3.   *Sincere questions* are aimed at understanding others.

           4.   *Counterfeit questions* are disguised attempts to send a message, not receive one.

      C.   *Paraphrasing* is feedback that restates the message the speaker sent.

           1.   Paraphrasing factual information includes summarizing facts, data, and details during personal or professional conversation.

           2.   Paraphrasing personal information includes thoughts, feelings and wants.

      D.   *Empathizing* is a style used to show that the listener is identifying with the speaker.

      E.   *Supporting* responses reveal the listener's solidarity with the speaker and reflects the listener's feelings about the speaker.

      F.   *Analyzing* is when the listener offers an interpretation of the speaker's message.

      G   *Evaluating* responses are when the listener appraises the speaker's thoughts or behaviors.

      H.   *Advising* is the most common reaction to another's problem and may be helpful or harmful.

Chapter 7: Summary

Listening is the most frequent form of communication, and good listening skills are more valued than good speaking skills. Listening is the process of making sense of others' spoken messages and is different from hearing, which is the physical process in which sound waves strike the eardrum and cause vibrations that are transmitted to the brain. Mindless listening occurs when we react to others' messages automatically and routinely. Mindful listening involves giving careful and thoughtful attention and responses to the messages we receive.

Reasons to listen include: to understand, to evaluate, to build and maintain relationships, and to help others. Listening fidelity describes the degree of congruence between what a listener understands and what the message-sender was attempting to communicate.

Listening carefully is a challenge, and there are several obstacles, including information overload, personal concerns, rapid thought, and noise. Furthermore, all listeners do not receive the same message, since physiological factors, social roles, cultural background, personal interests, and needs all shape and distort the raw data we hear into very different messages.

Most people possess one or more personal listening habits. Pseudolistening is imitation listening; one may give the appearance of listening but is not really doing so. Stage hogs are only interested in expressing their ideas. Selective listeners respond only to the parts of a speaker's remarks that interest them. People fill in the gaps in order to make listeners think they remember a whole story while they manufacture information to give a false impression. Insulated listening is avoiding hearing something. Defensive listening is when people take innocent comments as personal attacks. An ambusher listens carefully in order to collect information that will be used in an attack. Attending is a psychological process where one focuses intently on the message and both verbal and nonverbal cues. Understanding a message depends on knowing the basic rules of language, the source of the message, and the listener's mental abilities. Remembering is a function of the number of times the information is heard or repeated, how much information there is to store, and whether the information may be rehearsed or not. Responding is giving observable feedback to the speaker.

There are several types of listening responses. Silent listening is staying attentive and nonverbally responsive without offering any verbal feedback. Questioning occurs when the listener asks the speaker for additional information. Open questions allow for extended responses, while closed questions allow a limited range of answers. Sincere questions are aimed at understanding others, while counterfeit questions are really disguised attempts to send a message, not to receive one. Paraphrasing is feedback that restates in the listener's words, the message that they think the speaker sent. Empathizing is a response style used to show that the listener is identifying with a speaker. Supporting responses reveal the listener's solidarity with the speaker's situation. Analyzing a situation is when the listener offers an interpretation of a speaker's message. Evaluating responses appraise the sender's thoughts or behaviors in some way. Advising is the most common reaction to another's problem.

Chapter 7: Key Terms

For each of these terms, define the term, give an example, and explain the significance of the term.

1. Advising

2. Ambushing

3. Analyzing

4. Attending

5. Closed questions

6. Counterfeit questions

7. Defensive listening

8. Empathizing

9. Evaluating

10. Filling in gaps

11. Hearing

12. Insulated listening

13. Listening

14. Listening fidelity

15. Mindful listening

16. Mindless listening

17. Open questions

18. Paraphrasing

19. Pseudolistening

20. Questioning

21. Remembering

22. Responding

23. Selective listening

24. Silent listening

25. Sincere questions

26. Stage hogging

27. Supporting

28. Understanding

Chapter 7: Review Questions

These questions are designed to help you better understand the concepts from this chapter and also allow you the opportunity to put the information into your own words. For practice true/false and multiple-choice questions, please refer to the course website.

1. What are the four different reasons for listening, and what are the corresponding sets of attitudes and skills for each?

2. Identify and describe the four obstacles, or barriers, to effective listening.

3. Identify and describe the seven types of poor listening habits.

4. What are the five components of listening, in order?

5. Identify and define the eight types of listening responses.

Chapter 7: Thinking Outside the Box: Synthesizing Your Knowledge

These questions are designed to help connect the course material from previous chapters.

1. How is listening fidelity affected by attributions and patterns of thought that occur during the process of decoding messages (Chapter 2)?

2. As explained in Chapter 1, noise is one of the components of the model of communication. What is the relationship between noise and the barriers to effective listening?

Chapter 7: Answers to Review Questions

1. What are the four different reasons for listening, and what are the corresponding sets of attitudes and skills for each?

   (1) To understand is to retain information. (2) To evaluate means to judge the quality of the message. (3) To build and maintain relationships, which occurs through effective listening as it helps builds better relationships, according to research. (4) To help others, because when people listen to others with understanding and concern, they can gain different and useful perspectives for solving problems.

2. Identify and describe the four obstacles, or barriers, to effective listening.

   (1) Information overload is a result of a barrage of messages, as people often choose to listen mindlessly instead of mindfully. (2) Personal concerns can hinder listening; people are often distracted by matters of more immediate concern than the messages others are sending. (3) Rapid thought can get in the way of careful listening, because our minds are active; the brain works faster than a person can speak. (4) Noise presents both physical and psychological distractions.

3. Identify and describe the seven types of poor listening habits.

   (1) Pseudolistening is an imitation of actual listening. (2) Stage hogs are interested only in expressing their ideas and don't care about what anyone else has to say. (3) Selective listening is when listeners respond only to the parts of a message that interest them. (4) Fill in gaps is what people do when they like to think that they remember a whole story and manufacture information to complete the picture. (5) Insulated listening is when someone fails to hear or acknowledge something in a message. (6) Defensive listening is when someone takes innocent comments as personal attacks. (7) Ambushing is listening carefully but only to gather information to later use against the speaker.

4. What are the five components of listening, in order?

   (1) Hearing is the physiological aspect of listening. (2) Attending is the psychological process of listening and is part of the process of selection. (3) Understanding is composed of several elements: awareness of the rules of the language, knowledge of the source of the message, and mental ability. (4) Remembering is the ability to recall information. (5) Responding is the final step of the listening process and involves offering feedback to the speaker.

5. Identify and define the eight types of listening responses.

   (1) Silent listening is staying attentive and responsive nonverbally. (2) Questioning occurs when the listener asks the speaker for additional information. (3) Paraphrasing is feedback that restates the message the speaker sent. (4) Empathizing is a style used to show that the listener is identifying with the speaker. (5) Supporting responses reveal the listener's solidarity with the speaker and reflect the listener's

feelings about the speaker. (6) Analyzing is when the listener offers an interpretation of the speaker's message. (7) Evaluating responses are when the listener appraises the sender's thoughts or behaviors. (8) Advising is the most common reaction to another's problem and may be helpful or harmful.

Chapter 7: Answers to Thinking Outside the Box

1. How is listening fidelity affected by attributions and patterns of thought that occur during the process of decoding messages (Chapter 2)?

   Listening fidelity is a term used to describe the degree of congruence between what a listener understands and what the sender was attempting to communicate. When decoding messages, the potential for misunderstandings for communicators from different cultural backgrounds is great. Attribution is the process of making sense of another's behavior, and since most behavior is ambiguous and may have several interpretations, the attribution process can lead to making faulty interpretations. Also, patterns of thought vary in the way members of a culture are taught to think, and reason shapes they way they interpret others' messages.

2. As explained in Chapter 1, noise is one of the components of the model of communication. What is the relationship between noise and the barriers to effective listening?

   Noise is anything that interferes with the transmission and reception of a message. External noise includes different kinds of distractions that are outside the receiver that make it difficult to hear. Noise also presents both physical and psychological distractions. Physiological noise involves biological factors that interfere with reception. Psychological noise refers to cognitive factors that lessen the effectiveness of communication. The barriers to effective listening include psychological factors such as information overload, personal concerns, and rapid thought. Information overload is a result of a barrage of messages; people often choose to listen mindlessly instead of mindfully. Personal concerns can hinder listening; people are often distracted by matters of more immediate concern than the messages others are sending. Rapid thought can get in the way of careful listening, because our minds are active; the brain works faster than a person can speak.

Chapter 8: Emotions

SQ3R in Action

Generate an SQ3R chart for this chapter here:
http://www.teach-nology.com/web_tools/graphic_org/sq3r

Survey

Skim the title, key terms, chapter outline, objectives ("You should understand" and "You should be able to"), headings, tables, photos, cartoons, figures, charts, and items in the margin. Glance at the titles of the Focus on Research, Reflection, Film Clips, Self-Assessment, and Dark Side. At the end of each chapter, look over the Summary, Critical Thinking Probes, Ethical Challenges, Skill Builder, and Resources.

Question

Ask yourself questions. What do you know about these topics from your own life experiences and from other classes? Ask these six questions in each section: who, what, when, where, how, and why?

Read

Take one heading at a time and read to find the answers to the questions you've posed.

Recite

In your own words, say the answer aloud and then write it out.

Review

Review each section and then review the whole chapter. This is a good time to use the activities at the end of each chapter and the activities and the sample exams on the course website. Remember to periodically review the previous chapters as well.

Chapter 8: Outline

(Italicized words are key terms.)

I. Emotions are made up of several components.
    A. Physiological changes such as a churning stomach or tense jaw can occur when a person has strong emotions.
    B. Nonverbal reactions include blushing, perspiring, and behavior such as posture, gestures, or different vocal tone and rate.
    C. Cognitive interpretations affect emotions, as the mind plays an important role in determining how we feel.
    D. Verbal expressions are used to display emotions.

II. There are many influences on emotional expression; we are all born with the ability to reveal emotions, but over time one develops differences in emotional expression.
 A. Personality—There is a clear relationship between personality and the way people experience and communicate emotions.
 B. Culture plays a role in the way we express emotion as well as how we interpret the emotions of others.
 C. Gender roles often shape the ways in which men and women experience and express their emotions.
 D. Social conventions and roles affect the expression of direct emotions.
 E. Fear of self-disclosure exists because there are risks involved with self-disclosing, and unpleasant consequences may occur.
 F. *Emotional Contagion* is the process by which emotions are transferred from one person to another.

III. There are several guidelines for the healthy expression of emotions. Recognize your feelings—One must be able to distinguish and label one's emotions.
 A. Chose the best language in order to truly be expressive about emotions.
  1. Describe your feelings using metaphorical language.
  2. Describe what you would like to do.
 B. Share multiple feelings; while it is common to experience more than one emotion at a time, we usually only express one emotion.
 C. Recognize the difference between feeling and acting.
 D. Accept responsibility for your feelings by not blaming others for how you feel.
 E. Choose the best time and place to express your feelings. Usually it is better to delay expressing feelings or even never express feelings, depending on the situation.

IV. Managing difficult emotions is difficult, as distorted self-perceptions can generate emotions that interfere with effective communication.
 A. *Facilitative emotions* contribute to effective functioning, while *debilitative emotions* hinder or prevent effective performance, an example of which is *communication apprehension,* or feelings of anxiety that some people experience at the prospect of communicating in unfamiliar contexts.
  1. Debilitative emotions are more intense than facilitative.
  2. Debilitative feelings also have an extended duration.
 B. Thoughts cause feelings; a rational emotive approach to changing feelings is to change unproductive thinking, which lies in the pattern of thought that manifests itself through *self-talk*, the nonvocal internal monologue that is our process of thinking.
 C. Irrational thinking and debilitative emotions come from accepting irrational thoughts or fallacies.
  1. *Fallacy of perfection* is the thought that a competent communicator should be able to handle any situation with complete confidence and skill.
  2. *Fallacy of approval* is the mistaken belief that it is vital to obtain everyone's approval.

3. *Fallacy of should* is the inability to distinguish between what is and what should be.
4. *Fallacy of overgeneralization* occurs when a person bases a belief on a limited amount of evidence.
5. *Fallacy of causation* is the belief that one should not do anything that will cause harm or inconvenience to others because it will cause undesirable feelings.
6. *Fallacy of catastrophic expectations* occurs when one assume that if something bad can happen then it will; catastrophic thinking often takes the form of *rumination,* which is the presence of recurrent thoughts not demanded by the immediate environment.

D. Minimizing debilitative emotions can be achieved by monitoring emotional reactions.
1. Note the activating event so that you are aware of the trigger which may be specific people, types of individuals, settings, or topics of conversation.
2. Record your self-talk so that you are able to analyze the thoughts that link the trigger and your feelings.
3. Dispute your irrational beliefs by choosing an alternate belief that is more sensible.

Chapter 8: Summary

Emotions have several components. Physiological changes occur when a person has strong emotions. Nonverbal reactions to emotions can also cause external physical changes, such as blushing or perspiring. Cognitive interpretations occur because the mind plays an important role in how we feel. Verbal expression is sometimes necessary to express feelings. Influences on emotional expression include personality, culture, gender, social convention and roles, fear of self-disclosure, and emotional contagion.

Expressing emotion constructively is key to good health and to improving relationships. The first step to effectively expressing emotions is to recognize your feelings. Choosing the best language to describe feelings is important to the process of expressing feelings. It is also important to express multiple feelings, since oftentimes one experiences several emotions at once. Recognizing the difference between feeling and acting is important. Accept responsibility for your feelings, and do not blame others for the way you feel. Choose the best time and place to express your feelings.

At times we view ourselves in a distorted fashion. Facilitative emotions contribute to effective functioning, while debilitative emotions hinder or prevent effective performance. Communication apprehension is when one feels anxious at the thought of communicating in an unfamiliar or difficult context and is an example of debilitative emotions. One must find a way to rid oneself of debilitative feelings while keeping facilitative emotions; the rational emotive approach can do that. This approach is based on the idea that the key to changing feelings is to change unproductive thinking. Self-talk is the nonvocal internal monologue that is our process of thinking and is the key to understanding and changing feelings.

Many debilitative feelings come from accepting a number of irrational thoughts called fallacies. The fallacy of perfection is the false belief that a worthwhile communicator should be able to handle any situation with complete confidence and skills and that imperfections are unacceptable. The fallacy of approval is the mistaken belief that is vital to obtain everyone's approval to the extent of sacrificing their own principles and happiness. The fallacy of should is a huge source of unhappiness, since it is the inability to distinguish what is and what should be. The fallacy of overgeneralization occurs when a person bases a belief on a limited amount of evidence. The fallacy of causation causes people to believe they should do nothing that can hurt or in any way inconvenience others because it will cause undesirable feelings. The fallacy of catastrophic expectations is the mistaken belief that if something bad can happen, it will. Catastrophic thinking often manifests as rumination, or recurrent thoughts not demanded by the immediate environment.

Irrational thinking can be overcome by a simple approach. The first step is to recognize debilitative emotions. The second step is to note the activating event in order to figure out what triggers these emotions. The third step is to record self-talk in order to identify the thoughts that lead to the debilitative feelings. The fourth step is to dispute any irrational beliefs.

Chapter 8: Key Terms

For each of these terms, define the term, give an example, and explain the significance of the term.

1. Communication apprehension

2. Debilitative emotions

3. Emotional contagion

4. Facilitative emotions

5. Fallacy of approval

6. Fallacy of catastrophic expectations

7. Fallacy of causation

8. Fallacy of helplessness

9. Fallacy of overgeneralization

10. Fallacy of perfection

11. Fallacy of should

12. Rumination

13. Self-talk

Chapter 8: Review Questions

These questions are designed to help you better understand the concepts from this chapter and also allow you the opportunity to put the information into your own words. For practice true/false and multiple-choice questions, please refer to the course website.

1. Explain the four components that make up emotions.

2. Identify and explain the six influences on emotional expression.

3. Explain the four guidelines for the healthy expression of emotions.

4. Identify and describe the six fallacies of irrational thinking.

5. What are some strategies that can be used to minimize debilitative emotions?

Chapter 8: Thinking Outside the Box: Synthesizing Your Knowledge

These questions are designed to help connect the course material from previous chapters.

1. How may culture (Chapter 2) impact an individual's expression of emotions?

2. How does communication competence (Chapter 1) relate to the healthy expression of emotions?

Chapter 8: Answers to Review Questions

1. Explain the four components that make up emotions.

   Physiological changes such as a churning stomach or tense jaw can occur when a person has strong emotions. Nonverbal reactions include blushing, perspiring, and behavior such as posture, gestures, or different vocal tone and rate. Cognitive interpretations affect emotions, as the mind plays an important role in determining how we feel. Verbal expressions are used to display emotions.

2. Identify and explain the six influences on emotional expression.

   (1) Personality—There is a clear relationship between personality and the way people experience and communicate emotions. (2) Culture plays a role in the way we express emotion as well as how we interpret the emotions of others. (3) Gender roles often shape the ways in which men and women experience and express their emotions. (4) Social conventions and roles affect the expression of direct emotions. (5) Fear of self-disclosure exists because there are risks involved with self-disclosing, and unpleasant consequences may occur. (6) Emotional contagion is the process by which emotions are transferred from one person to another.

3. Explain the four guidelines for the healthy expression of emotions.

   (1) Choose the best language in order to truly be expressive about emotions by using metaphors and description. Share multiple feelings; while it is common to experience more than one emotion at a time, we usually only express one emotion. (2) Recognize the difference between feeling and acting. (3) Accept responsibility for your feelings by not blaming others for how you feel. (4) Choose the best time and place to express your feelings.

4. Identify and describe the six fallacies of irrational thinking.

   The fallacy of perfection is the thought that a competent communicator should be able to handle any situation with complete confidence and skill. The fallacy of approval is the mistaken belief that it is vital to obtain everyone's approval. The fallacy of should is the inability to distinguish between what is and what should be. The fallacy of overgeneralization occurs when a person bases a belief on a limited amount of evidence. The fallacy of causation is the belief that one should not do anything that will cause harm or inconvenience to others because it will cause undesirable feelings. And last, the fallacy of catastrophic expectations occurs when one assume that if something bad can happen then it will, and catastrophic thinking often takes the form of rumination, or recurrent thoughts not demanded by the immediate environment.

5. What are some strategies that can be used to minimize debilitative emotions?

First, note the activating event so that you are aware of the trigger which may be specific people, types of individuals, settings, or topics of conversation. Second, record your self-talk so that you are able to analyze the thoughts that link the trigger and your feelings. And last, dispute your irrational beliefs by choosing an alternate belief that is more sensible.

Chapter 8: Answers to Thinking Outside the Box

1. How may culture (Chapter 2) impact an individual's expression of emotions?

There are many influences on emotional expression; we are all born with the ability to reveal emotions, but over time one develops differences in emotional expression. Culture plays a role in the way we express emotion as well as how we interpret the emotions of others. For example, in a low-context culture, language is used primarily to express thoughts, feelings, and ideas as directly as possible, which contrasts with a high-context culture, which relies heavily on subtle, often nonverbal cues to maintain social harmony. Individualistic cultures consider their primary responsibility to be to help themselves, while collectivistic cultures feel loyalties and obligations to an in-group, and personal emotions may therefore be muted. Power distance is the degree to which members of a society accept an unequal distribution of power; the less power one has, the less emotional expression may be appropriate.

2. How does communication competence (Chapter 1) relate to the healthy expression of emotions?

Communication competence is defined as communication that is both effective and appropriate. There is no single ideal or effective way to communicate or express emotions, as the definition of what is appropriate in a given situation varies considerably from one culture to another. Competence is situational, as communication competence is not absolute but exists in degrees or areas of competence. Because communication varies from one culture to another, competent emotional expression does as well. There are several guidelines for the healthy expression of emotions. Choose the best language in order to truly be expressive about emotions. Accept responsibility for your feelings by not blaming others for how you feel. Choose the best time and place to express your feelings; usually it is better to delay expressing feelings or even to never express feelings, depending on the situation.

Chapter 9: Dynamics of Interpersonal Relationships

SQ3R in Action

Generate an SQ3R chart for this chapter here:
http://www.teach-nology.com/web_tools/graphic_org/sq3r

Survey

. Skim the title, key terms, chapter outline, objectives ("You should understand" and "You should be able to"), headings, tables, photos, cartoons, figures, charts, and items in the margin. Glance at the titles of the Focus on Research, Reflection, Film Clips, Self-Assessment, and Dark Side. At the end of each chapter, look over the Summary, Critical Thinking Probes, Ethical Challenges, Skill Builder, and Resources.

Question

Ask yourself questions. What do you know about these topics from your own life experiences and from other classes? Ask these six questions in each section: who, what, when, where, how, and why?

Read

Take one heading at a time and read to find the answers to the questions you've posed.

Recite

In your own words, say the answer aloud and then write it out.

Review

Review each section and then review the whole chapter. This is a good time to use the activities at the end of each chapter and the activities and the sample exams on the course website. Remember to periodically review the previous chapters as well.

Chapter 9: Outline

(Italicized words are key terms.)

I.   We form relationships with some people and not with others, and we form relationships for interpersonal attraction and a desire for intimacy.
    A.   Different factors of attraction influence our choice of relational partners.
        1.   Appearance is especially important in the beginning of a relationship.
        2.   The similarity thesis states that similarities form the basis of relationships.

3. Complementarily is a factor, as differences strengthen a relationship when they are complementary so that each partner's characteristics satisfy the other's needs.

4. Some relationships are based on the economic model, called Social Exchange Theory, that we seek out people that can give us benefits, or rewards, while minimizing costs which are undesirable outcomes.

   a. *Comparison level* (CL) is the minimum standard of what behavior in a relationship is acceptable.

   b. *Comparison level of alternatives* (CLalt) is the standard that compares the rewards one receives in a current relationship and what can be expected in other situations.

5. Competency is another factor, as we like to be around people who are good at what they do.

6. Proximity matters, because we are likely to develop relationships with people with whom we frequently interact.

7. Disclosure involves sharing information and is a form of trust and respect that increases attractiveness as long as there is reciprocity, or receiving an amount and kind of information equivalent to what is revealed, and the timing is right.

8. Relational commitment involves a promise to remain in a relationship and to make the relationship successful.

B. Intimacy can be emotional, where one shares important feelings and information, or physical or intellectual sharing, where one exchanges ideas, or it can even come from shared activities.

   1. Gender and intimacy affect relationships, as women place a somewhat higher value on talking about personal matters as a measure of closeness while men are more likely to achieve closeness through shared activities.

   2. Intimacy varies from culture to culture, but these differences are becoming less prominent.

   3. Relational intimacy can be achieved through computer-mediated communication and may even be developed more quickly.

   4. There are limits of intimacy; on average, most people want four to six close, important relationships in their lives at any given time, with less than four relationships leading to a sense of social deprivation and more than six leading to diminishing returns.

C. *Relational commitment* involves a promise to remain in a relationship and to make that relationship successful.

II. Knapp's developmental models of interpersonal relationships include the beginning and ending of a relationship and should include *relational maintenance*, which is communication aimed at keeping relationships operating smoothly.

A. *Initiating* is the stage where the goals are to show that one is interested in making contact and demonstrating that one is a person worthy of talking to.

B. *Experimenting* is the stage after initiating, wherein we seek information about the other person, sometimes using small talk to find the information we seek.

C. *Intensifying* involves shared activities, spending increased amounts of time together, etc., and is marked by relational excitement and euphoria.

D. *Integrating* is when couples take on an identity as a social unit and their social circles merge.

E. *Bonding* is the stage where couples make symbolic public gestures about their relationship.

F. *Differentiating* is when the couple starts to reestablish individual identities and occurs when the relationship begins to experience the first feelings of stress.

G. *Circumscribing* stage is when communication between members decreases in quality and quantity.

H. *Stagnating* occurs when circumscribing continues and no new growth occurs.

I. *Avoiding* takes place when stagnation becomes too unpleasant and people begin creating distance between each other.

J. *Terminating* is the end of the relationship.

III. The dialectical perspective on relational dynamics is another way of explaining interaction in relationships and is focused on *dialectical tensions,* or conflicts that arise when two opposing or incompatible forces exist simultaneously.

A. The *integration-separation dialectic* embodies the conflicting desires for connection and independence.

1. The *connection-autonomy dialectic* is where we want to be close to others but also seek to be autonomous; it is an internal struggle.

2. The *inclusion-seclusion dialectic* is the external struggle between integration and separation.

B. The *stability-change dialectic* operates between partners and when they face others outside the relationship.

1. The *predictability-novelty dialectic* is the tension within a relationship that comes from intimate knowledge of someone that causes a lower level of passion.

2. The *conventionality-uniqueness dialectic* is the tension felt by people when they try to meet others' expectations.

C. The *expression-privacy dialectic*—Along with *intimacy*, we crave distance between ourselves and others.

1. *Openness-closedness dialectic* is the internal struggle between expression and privacy.

2. *Revelation-concealment dialectic* is the external expression of the conflict between openness and privacy.

D. Strategies for managing dialectical tensions include denial, disorientation, alternation, segmentation, balance, integration, recalibration, and reaffirmation.

IV. Relationships are maintained through communication, as relationships need ongoing maintenance to keep them successful and satisfying.

A. There are strategies for maintaining relationships and repairing damaged relationships.

1.   Through content-oriented and relational messages: content-oriented messages are informational in nature but also contain information about how the communicators feel about each other and are relational.
2.   The expression of relational messages is usually achieved nonverbally.
3.   *Metacommunication* describes messages that refer to other messages, as in when a couple discusses issues affecting their relationship and such messages are verbal.

B.   Relational maintenance strategies include positivity, openness, assurances, sharing tasks, and social networks.
C.   Repairing damaged relationships is challenging, as problems arise from outside or internal forces or from a relational transgression, which is when one partner violates the explicit or implicit terms of the relationship.
1.   Minor versus significant needs to be considered, as small doses of jealousy or anger or distance are not harmful while large amounts are.
2.   Social versus relational is another consideration, as some transgressions violate social rules shared by society, while others are relational and violate the unique norms constructed by the parties involved.
3.   Deliberate versus unintentional captures the notion that while some transgressions are unintentional others are deliberate.
4.   One-time versus incremental means that some transgressions occur in a single episode while others occur over time.

D.   Strategies for relational repair include discussing the violation and for the offending partner to offer an apology.
1.   The apology should consist of an acknowledgement of wrong-doing, a sincere apology, and some type of compensation.
2.   Forgiving transgressions is difficult, but it can be beneficial to both parties.

Chapter 9: Summary

We seek out relationships with some people and not with others and we form relationships for interpersonal attraction and a desire for intimacy. There are several factors that make someone attractive and influence our choice of relational partners. Appearance is especially important in the early stages of a relationship. The *similarity thesis* states that people seek similarity in a partner. We also seek people who have differences that are *complementary* and strengthen the relationship. The Social Exchange Theory posits that some relationships are based on the idea that we often seek people who can give us rewards (or outcomes that we desire) that are greater than or equal to the costs we encounter in dealing with them. There are two standards when dealing with rewards and costs. The first is the comparison level (CL) and is a minimum standard of what is acceptable; the second is the comparison level of alternatives (CLalt), or the standard that refers to a comparison between the rewards one receives in a current situation and what one can expect to receive in another situation. We are also drawn to people based on their proximity. Disclosure, or sharing private information, can increase attractiveness, though it is not guaranteed to do so; the keys to satisfying self-disclosure are reciprocity and timing.

The desire for intimacy is another reason we seek to form interpersonal relationships. Intimacy comes in different forms—physical, emotional, or intellectual—while shared activities is another type of intimacy. Many women think of sex as a way of expressing intimacy, but many men see sex as a way to create intimacy. Intimacy varies from one culture to another, though these differences are not as pronounced as they have been in the past. Intimacy is available through computer-mediated communication, and relational intimacy may even develop more quickly through CMC. There are limits to intimacy, as most people want four to six close important relationships in their lives at any given time. Fewer than four can lead to a sense of social deprivation, and more than six can result in diminishing returns.

Relational commitment involves a promise to remain in a relationship and to make that relationship successful. Commitment is important for every interpersonal relationship.

Mark Knapp developed one of the best known models of relational stages, but it does not include relational maintenance, which is communication aimed at keeping relationships operating smoothly and satisfactorily. Some researchers feel that relational maintenance should be included in any model of relational stages. The ten stages of Knapp's relational model are initiating, experimenting, intensifying, integrating, bonding, differentiating, circumscribing, stagnating, avoiding, and terminating.

Another way of looking at relationships is through dialectical tensions, which are conflicts that arise when two opposing or incompatible forces exist simultaneously. Integration-separation dialectic is the conflicting desire for connection and independence and shows up within a relationship. Internally, the struggle shows up in the connection-autonomy dialectic, where we want to be close to others but we seek independence at the same time. The tension between integration and separation occurs externally with the inclusion-seclusion dialectic, where a couple struggles to be involved with the outside world while being free of interference from others. The stability-change dialectic occurs between partners and when they face the outside world. The predictability-novel dialectic captures the tension of knowing everything about someone while experiencing lack of passion due to a lack of novelty. The conventionality-uniqueness dialectic occurs when people in a relationship face challenges to live up to the expectations of others. The expression-privacy dialectic is born out of our seemingly contradictory need for intimacy and space between ourselves and others. The openness-closedness dialectic is the internal expression of the struggle between expression and privacy, while revelation-concealment dialectic is the external expression. There are some strategies for managing dialectical tensions, including denial, disorientation, alternation, segmentation, balance, integration, recalibration and reaffirmation.

Relationships need ongoing maintenance, and there are strategies for maintaining relationships and for repairing damaged relationships. Messages are both content-oriented and relational, meaning that information isn't the only thing exchanged in messages, but the way the speaker feels about the recipient is also expressed. Relational messages are expressed mainly nonverbally, but there are some that are present in metacommunication, which is communication about communication. Verbal metacommunication is an essential ingredient in successful relationships and relational repair. There are five strategies for maintaining romantic relationships, which are positivity, openness, assurances, sharing tasks, and social networks.

Outside and internal forces can cause relationship problems, as can a relational transgression, which occurs when one partner violates the explicit or implicit terms of the relationship. Relational transgressions include such things as criticism, jealousy, or verbal hostility. The first step to repairing a transgression is to talk about the violation. A successful apology should include an explicit acknowledgement that the transgression was wrong, a sincere apology, and some type of compensation. Though forgiving a transgression is hard, forgiveness benefits both parties.

Chapter 9: Key Terms

For each of these terms, define the term, give an example, and explain the significance of the term.

1. Avoiding

2. Bonding

3. Circumscribing

4. Comparison level (CL)

5. Comparison level of alternatives (CLalt)

6. Connection-autonomy dialectic

7. Conventionality-uniqueness dialectic

8. Dialectical tensions

9. Differentiating

10. Experimenting

11. Expression-privacy dialectic

12. Inclusion-seclusion dialectic

13. Initiating

14. Integrating

15. Integration-separation dialectic

16. Intensifying

17. Intimacy

18. Metacommunication

19. Openness-closedness dialectic

20. Predictability-novelty dialectic

21. Relational commitment

22. Relational maintenance

23. Revelation-concealment dialectic

24. Stability-change dialectic

25. Stagnating

26. Terminating

Chapter 9: Review Questions

These questions are designed to help you better understand the concepts from this chapter and also allow you the opportunity to put the information into your own words. For practice true/false and multiple-choice questions, please refer to the course website.

1. Identify some of the different factors that influence attraction and the choice of relational partners.

2. Explain the Social Exchange Theory as it relates to relationships.

3. Explain how gender affects intimacy and relationships.

4. Identify and explain Knapp's developmental models of interpersonal relationships.

5. Explain the dialectical perspectives on relational dynamics and identify the three sets of dialectical tensions.

Chapter 9: Thinking Outside the Box: Synthesizing Your Knowledge

These questions are designed to help connect the course material from previous chapters.

1. What are the factors that influence intimacy development through computer-mediated communication (Chapter 1)?

2. What is the role of self-disclosure (Chapter 3) as it relates to the Relational Stage Model?

Chapter 9: Answers to Review Questions

1. Identify some of the different factors that influence attraction and the choice of relational partners.

   (1) Appearance is especially important in the beginning of a relationship. (2) The similarity thesis states that similarities form the basis of relationships. (3) Complementarily is a factor, as differences strengthen a relationship when they are complementary so that each partner's characteristics satisfy the other's needs. (4) Some relationships are based on the economic model, called Social Exchange Theory, that we seek out people that can give us benefits, or rewards, while minimizing costs, which are undesirable outcomes. (5) Competency is another factor, as we like to be around people who are good at what they do. (6) Proximity matters because we are likely to develop relationships with people with whom we frequently interact. (7) Disclosure involves sharing information and is a form of trust and respect that increases attractiveness as long as there is reciprocity, or receiving an amount and kind of information equivalent to what is revealed, and the timing is right. (8) Relational commitment involves a promise to remain in a relationship and to make the relationship successful.

2. Explain the Social Exchange Theory as it relates to relationships.

   The Social Exchange Theory is based on the economic model which posits that we seek out people that can give us benefits, or rewards, while minimizing costs, which are undesirable outcomes. Comparison level (CL) is the minimum standard of what behavior in a relationship is acceptable. Comparison level of alternatives (CLalt) is the standard that compares the rewards one receives in a current relationship and what can be expected in other situations.

3. Explain how gender affects intimacy and relationships.

   Gender and intimacy affect relationships, as women place a somewhat higher value on talking about personal matters as a measure of closeness, whereas men are more likely to achieve closeness through shared activities.

4. Identify and explain Knapp's developmental models of interpersonal relationships.

   Initiating is the stage where the goals are to show that one is interested in making contact and demonstrating that one is a person worthy of talking to. Experimenting is the stage after initiating in which we seek information about the other person, sometimes using small talk to find the information we seek. Intensifying involves shared activities, spending increased amounts of time together, etc., and is marked by relational excitement and euphoria. Integrating is when couples take on an identity as a social unit and their social circles merge. Bonding is the stage where couples make symbolic public gestures about their relationship. Differentiating is when the couple starts to reestablish individual identities and occurs when the relationship begins to experience the first feelings of stress. The circumscribing stage is when communication between members decreases in quality and quantity. Stagnating occurs when circumscribing continues and no new growth occurs. Avoiding takes place when stagnation becomes too unpleasant and people begin creating distance between each other. Terminating is ending the relationship.

5. Explain the dialectical perspectives on relational dynamics and identify the three sets of dialectical tensions.

   Dialectical Theory is a way of explaining interaction in relationships that is focused on dialectical tensions or conflicts that arise when two opposing or incompatible forces exist simultaneously. The integration-separation dialectic embodies the conflicting desires for connection and independence. The stability-change dialectic operates between partners and when they face others outside the relationship. The expression-privacy dialectic captures the tension that comes with intimacy, that we also want distance between ourselves and others.

Chapter 9: Answers to Thinking Outside the Box

1. What are the factors that influence intimacy development through computer-mediated communication (Chapter 1)?

   Intimacy develops through the sharing of emotions, important feelings, and information, and also may include intellectual sharing where one exchanges ideas. One context where relational intimacy can be achieved is through computer-mediated communication. Research suggests that intimacy may even be developed more quickly online. Computer-mediated communication can increase both the amount and the quality of interpersonal communication, since it is easier than face-to-face communication. Disinhibition is the tendency to transmit messages without considering the consequence, particularly through the volunteering personal information that might normally not be expressed.

2. What is the role of self-disclosure (Chapter 3) as it relates to the Relational Stage Model?

   Self-disclosure is defined by honesty, depth, availability of information, and context of sharing; furthermore, it has the self as subject, is intentional, is directed at another person, is honest, is revealing, contains information generally unavailable from other sources, and gains much of its intimate nature from the context in which it is expressed. There are benefits, which are highlighted during the stages of relational development, and risks, associated with relational decline, of self-disclosure; neither complete privacy nor complete disclosure is desirable. The stages of initiating, experimenting, intensifying, integrating, and bonding are characterized by self-disclosure. The stages of relational decline: differentiating, circumscribing, stagnating, avoiding, and terminating are characterized by the decrease of self-disclosure.

Chapter 10: Communication Climate

SQ3R in Action

Generate an SQ3R chart for this chapter here:
http://www.teach-nology.com/web_tools/graphic_org/sq3r

Survey

Skim the title, key terms, chapter outline, objectives ("You should understand" and "You should be able to"), headings, tables, photos, cartoons, figures, charts, and items in the margin. Glance at the titles of the Focus on Research, Reflection, Film Clips, Self-Assessment, and Dark Side. At the end of each chapter, look over the Summary, Critical Thinking Probes, Ethical Challenges, Skill Builder, and Resources.

Question

Ask yourself questions. What do you know about these topics from your own life experiences and from other classes? Ask these six questions in each section: who, what, when, where, how, and why?

Read

Take one heading at a time and read to find the answers to the questions you've posed.

Recite

In your own words, say the answer aloud and then write it out.

Review

Review each section and then review the whole chapter. This is a good time to use the activities at the end of each chapter and the activities and the sample exams on the course website. Remember to periodically review the previous chapters as well.

Chapter 10: Outline

<u>(Italicized words are key terms.)</u>

I. *Communication climate* refers to the social tone of a relationship and involves the way people feel about each other as they carry out activities.

II. Communication climates develop by the degree to which people see themselves as valued.

   A. *Confirming communication* refers to the three positive types of messages that have the best chance of being perceived as confirming.

   1. Recognition—The most fundamental act of confirmation is to recognize the other person.

2. Acknowledging the ideas and feelings of others is a stronger form of confirmation than simple recognition.

3. Endorsement means you agree with the speaker and is the highest form of confirming.

B. *Disagreeing messages* lie between confirming and disconfirming and communicate that the other person is wrong; there are three types of disagreement.

1. *Argumentativeness* is presenting and defending positions on issues while attacking positions taken by others.

2. *Complaining* is a way to register dissatisfaction without arguing.

3. *Aggressiveness* is the most destructive way to disagree with another person.

C. *Disconfirming communication* dismisses the value of a person; there are seven types of disconfirming response.

1. *Impervious responses* fail to acknowledge the other person's communicative attempt.

2. *Interrupting responses* occur when one person begins to speak before the other is through making a point.

3. *Irrelevant responses* are totally unrelated to what the other person was saying.

4. *Tangential responses* acknowledge the other person's communication, but the acknowledgement is used to steer the conversation in a new direction.

5. *Impersonal responses* are monologues filled with impersonal, intellectualized, and generalized statements so the speaker never interacts with the other individual on a personal level.

6. *Ambiguous* responses contain a message with more than one meaning.

7. *Incongruous responses* contain two messages that seem to deny or contradict each other, one at the verbal level and one at the nonverbal level.

D. *Defensiveness* is the process of protecting our *presenting self.*

1. Presenting self consists of all of the parts of the image you want to present to the world.

2. Our *face* is the side of ourselves we try to project to others.

3. *Face-threatening acts* are messages that seem to challenge the image we want to project.

E. Climate patterns occur, and once a *communication climate* is formed, it can take on a life of its own, which can be represented as a *spiral.*

III. Creating positive climates can be achieved through the use of strategies that can increase the odds of expressing yourself in ways that lead to positive relational climates.

A. Reducing defensiveness can occur by sending supportive rather than defense-provoking messages.

1. *Description,* rather than *evaluation,* is a way to offer your thoughts, feelings, and wants without judging the listener.

2. *Controlling communication* versus *problem orientation*— Controlling communication occurs when a sender seems to be

imposing a solution on the receiver with little regard for the receiver's needs or interests, while in problem orientation, communicators focus on finding a solution that satisfies both their own needs and those of others involved.

3. *Strategy* versus *spontaneity*—Strategy can be used to characterize defense-arousing messages in which speakers hide their ulterior motives, while spontaneity contrasts this behavior by being honest with others rather than manipulating them.

4. *Neutrality* versus *empathy*—Neutrality describes a behavior that arouses defensiveness due to its lack of concern for the welfare of another, while empathy provides support by accepting another's feelings.

5. *Superiority* versus *equality*—Patronizing messages are conveyed by people who feel superior due to possessing more talent or knowledge, and that irritates receivers, whereas speakers can achieve equality by communicating that although they may have greater talent in certain areas, they see others as having just as much worth as themselves.

6. *Certainty* versus *provisionalism*—Individuals who insist that they are right project the defense-arousing behavior of certainty, while provisionalism is when people may have strong opinions but are willing to acknowledge that they may not be right.

B. When offering constructive criticism, there are certain attitudes and skills that are especially helpful.

1. Check your motives, since there are times when telling others what you think, feel, or want is primarily for your own good, not theirs.

2. Choose a good time; ideally, it is best to wait for a time or arrange one when both parties can calmly and rationally discuss the issue of concern.

3. Buffer negatives with positives, using the *sandwich method,* which buffers criticism with praise and is effective because it helps the recipient perceive the comments as constructive and well-intentioned.

4. Follow-up is important so as to acknowledge positive changes which resulted from constructive criticism.

IV. To transform a negative climate, there are two alternating ways of reacting to negative communication.

A. First, seek more information.

1. Ask for specifics.-Request more specific information from the sender.

2. Guess about the specifics. When the critic is unable to provide specific details, guess at the specifics, asking the critic if your guesses are correct.

3. Paraphrase the speaker's ideas using reflective listening skills; this is especially good in helping others solve their problems.

4. Ask what the critic wants. If the critic's demand is not obvious, you will need to do some investigating.

5.   Ask about the consequences of your behavior to find out exactly what troublesome consequences your behavior has for the critic.

6.   Ask what else is wrong; by asking about other complaints, actual problems can be uncovered.

B.   Agreeing with the critic is another strategy. There is virtually no situation in which you cannot honestly accept the other person's point of view and still maintain your position, as there are several different types of agreement.

1. Agree with the truth when the person's criticism is factually correct.

2. Agree with the odds which brings hidden agendas into the open for resolution and also helps you become aware of some possibly previously unconsidered consequences of your actions.

3. Agree in principle, which allows you to accept the principle upon which the criticism is based and still behave as you have been.

4. Agree with the critic's perception by agreeing with the critic's right to perceive things their way; you acknowledge the reasonableness of their perceptions even though you don't agree or wish to change your behavior.

Chapter 10: Summary

Confirming communication is a term that describes messages that convey valuing, while disconfirming messages signal a lack of regard. Communication climate refers to the social tone of a relationship and involves the way people feel about each other. Confirming messages include recognition, acknowledgement, and endorsement.

Disagreeing messages are in between confirming and disconfirming messages; a disagreeing message indicates that the communicator is wrong. Argumentativeness, as defined by communication researchers, is presenting and defending positions on issues while attacking positions taken by others. Complaining is a way for communicators to register dissatisfaction without arguing. Aggressiveness is the most destructive way to disagree with another person.

Disconfirming messages are damaging, since they implicitly deny the value of another person. There are several types of disconfirming responses. An impervious response fails to acknowledge the other's communicative attempt. An interrupting response occurs when one person begins to speak before the other is through making a point. An irrelevant response is one that is totally unrelated to what the other person was saying. A tangential response acknowledges the other person's communication but in such a way as to steer the conversation in a new direction. An impersonal response is where the speaker responds with impersonal, intellectualized, and generalized statements. Ambiguous responses contain messages with more than one meaning. An incongruous response contains two messages that seem to deny or contradict each other, one at the verbal level and one at the nonverbal level.

Face-threatening acts are messages that seem to challenge the image we want to project. Defensiveness is the process of protecting our presenting self and is interactive, with all communicators contributing to the climate of a relationship.

Climate patterns can be positive or negative. A spiral is a reciprocal pattern and be can positive or negative, with confirming or disconfirming behavior being responded to in kind. There are strategies that can increase the odds of creating a positive relational climate. An evaluation is a defense-arousing message that judges the other person, usually in a negative way, and can be replaced by using description, a way to offer thoughts, wants, and feelings without judging the listener. Another defense-provoking message is controlling communication, which involves some attempt to control another person. Problem orientation is an alternative communication to controlling, and the focus is on finding a solution that satisfies everyone involved. Strategy characterizes defense-arousing messages in which speakers hide their ulterior motives, while spontaneity is being honest with others instead of manipulating them. Neutrality, or indifference, is another defense-arousing behavior, while empathy helps rid communication of indifference. Superiority creates a defensive climate by sending patronizing messages to people who possess less knowledge or talent than we do. Equality can be projected even if the speaker possesses more knowledge or talent than the receivers. Individuals who project certainty regard their own opinions as truth while dismissing the ideas of others. In order to avoid a defensive response, a communicator can replace certainty with provisionalism, which allows for strong opinions but allows the communicator to acknowledge that another position may be reasonable.

When offering constructive criticism, certain attitudes and skills are necessary. First, one should check the motives for offering constructive criticism. The goal is to offer information that helps the other person and preserves the relationship. One should also choose a good time to offer constructive criticism. Another method is to buffer negatives with positives, also known as the sandwich method, where a critical comment is sandwiched between two positive comments. Finally, one should follow up and acknowledge the positive changes that occurred due to the constructive criticism.

There are two simple ways to transform negative climates. The first way is to seek more information by asking for specifics, guessing about specifics, paraphrasing the speaker's ideas, asking the critic what he wants, asking about the consequences of your behavior, or asking what else is wrong. The second way is to agree with the critic. When agreeing with the critic, one can agree with the truth, agree with the odds, agree in principle, or agree with the critic's perception.

Chapter 10: Key Terms

For each of these terms, define the term, give an example, and explain the significance of the term.

1. Aggressiveness

2. Ambiguous response

3. Argumentativeness

4. Certainty

5. Communication climate

6. Complaining

7. Confirming communication

8. Controlling communication

9. Defensiveness

10. Description

11. Disagreeing messages

12. Disconfirming communication

13. Empathy

14. Equality

15. Evaluation

16. Face

17. Face-threatening acts

18. Impersonal response

19. Impervious response

20. Incongruous response

21. Interrupting response

22. Irrelevant response

23. Neutrality

24. Presenting self

25. Problem orientation

26. Provisionalism

27. Sandwich method

28. Spiral

29. Spontaneity

30. Strategy

31. Superiority

32. Tangential response

Chapter 10: Review Questions

These questions are designed to help you better understand the concepts from this chapter and also allow you the opportunity to put the information into your own words. For practice true/false and multiple-choice questions, please refer to the course website.

1. What are the three levels of message confirmation?

2. Describe disagreeing messages and the three types of them.

3. Identify and describe the ways that one can respond to disconfirming messages.

4. When offering constructive criticism, what are the certain attitudes and skills that are necessary?

5. To foster a positive communication climate, what are the different ways that one can agree with a critic?

Chapter 10: Thinking Outside the Box: Synthesizing Your Knowledge

These questions are designed to help connect the course material from previous chapters.

1. How are disconfirming messages similar to some of the poor listening habits (Chapter 7)?

2. How are relational dialectics (Chapter 9) similar to the opposing forces that characterize confirming and disconfirming climates?

Chapter 10: Answers to Review Questions

1. What are the three levels of message confirmation?

   Recognition is the most fundamental act of confirmation. Acknowledging the ideas and feelings of others is a stronger form of confirmation than simple recognition. Endorsement means you agree with the speaker and is the highest form of confirming.

2. Describe disagreeing messages and the three types of them.

   Disagreeing messages lie between confirming and disconfirming ones and communicate that the other person is wrong. There are three types of disagreement. First, argumentativeness is presenting and defending positions on issues while attacking positions taken by others. Second, complaining is a way to register dissatisfaction without arguing. Third, aggressiveness is the most destructive way to disagree with another person.

3. Identify and describe the seven types of disconfirming responses.

   An impervious response fails to acknowledge the other's communicative attempt. Interrupting response occurs when one person begins to speak before the other is through making a point. An irrelevant response is one that is totally unrelated to what the other person was saying. A tangential response acknowledges the other person's communication but in such a way as to steer the conversation in a new direction. Impersonal response is where the speaker responds with impersonal, intellectualized, and generalized statements. Ambiguous responses contain messages with more than one meaning. An incongruous response contains two messages that seem to deny or contradict each other, one at the verbal level and one at the nonverbal level.

4. When offering constructive criticism, what are the certain attitudes and skills that are necessary?

First, one should check the motives for offering constructive criticism. The goal is to offer information that helps the other person and preserves the relationship. One should also choose a good time to offer constructive criticism. Another method is to buffer negatives with positives, also known as the sandwich method, where a critical comment is sandwiched between two positive comments. Finally, one should follow up and acknowledge the positive changes that occurred due to the constructive criticism.

5. To foster a positive communication climate, what are the different ways that one can agree with a critic?

(1) Agree with the truth when the person's criticism is factually correct. (2) Agree with the odds which brings hidden agendas into the open for resolution and also helps you become aware of some possibly previously unconsidered consequences of your actions. (3) Agree in principle, which allows you to accept the principle upon which the criticism is based and still behave as you have been. (4) Agree with the critic's perception; by agreeing with the critic's right to perceive things their way, you acknowledge the reasonableness of their perceptions even though you don't agree or wish to change your behavior.

Chapter 10: Answers to Thinking Outside the Box

1. How are disconfirming messages similar to some of the poor listening habits (Chapter 7)?

Disconfirming messages dismiss the value of a person, whereas poor listening habits keep people from understanding others' messages. Impervious responses fail to acknowledge the other person's communicative attempt. Stage hogs are interested only in expressing their ideas and don't care about what anyone else has to say. Insulated listening is when someone fails to hear or acknowledge something in a message. Interrupting responses occur when one person begins to speak before the other is through making a point. Defensive listening is when someone takes innocent comments as personal attacks. Ambushing is listening carefully but only to gather information to later use against the speaker. Irrelevant responses are totally unrelated to what the other person was saying. Tangential responses acknowledge the other person's communication, but the acknowledgement is used to steer the conversation in a new direction. Selective listening is when listeners respond only to the parts of a message that interest them. Impersonal responses are monologues filled with impersonal, intellectualized, and generalized statements so the speaker never interacts with the other on a personal level. Ambiguous responses contain a message with more than one meaning. Incongruous responses contain two messages that seem to deny or contradict each other, one at the verbal level and one at the nonverbal level.

2. How are relational dialectics (Chapter 9) similar to the opposing forces that characterize confirming and disconfirming climates?

    The dialectical perspectives on relational dynamics are another way of explaining interaction in relationships and are focused on dialectical tensions or conflicts that arise when two opposing or incompatible forces exist simultaneously. Climate patterns can be positive or negative and are characterized by two opposing forces as well.

Chapter 11: Managing Conflict

SQ3R in Action

Generate an SQ3R chart for this chapter here:
http://www.teach-nology.com/web_tools/graphic_org/sq3r

Survey

Skim the title, key terms, chapter outline, objectives ("You should understand" and "You should be able to"), headings, tables, photos, cartoons, figures, charts, and items in the margin. Glance at the titles of the Focus on Research, Reflection, Film Clips, Self-Assessment, and Dark Side. At the end of each chapter, look over the Summary, Critical Thinking Probes, Ethical Challenges, Skill Builder, and Resources.

Question

Ask yourself questions. What do you know about these topics from your own life experiences and from other classes? Ask these six questions in each section: who, what, when, where, how, and why?

Read

Take one heading at a time and read to find the answers to the questions you've posed.

Recite

In your own words, say the answer aloud and then write it out.

Review

Review each section and then review the whole chapter. This is a good time to use the activities at the end of each chapter and the activities and the sample exams on the course website. Remember to periodically review the previous chapters as well.

Chapter 11: Outline

(Italicized words are key terms.)

I.   *Conflict* is an expressed struggle between at least two interdependent parties who perceive incompatible goals, scarce resources, and interference from the other party in achieving their goals.

     A.   Expressed struggle captures the notion that conflict does not exist unless all the people involved know that the disagreement exists even if the expressed struggle is not verbalized.

     B.   Perceived incompatible goals is a situation where it seems as if the goals of those involved are mutually exclusive, but that is not always the case, as mutually satisfying answers can be agreed upon.

        C.   Perceived scarce resources occurs when people believe there are not enough resources, such as time, money, affection and space to go around.

        D.   Interdependence is another feature that captures the notion that people in a conflict are dependent upon each other.

        E.   Inevitability addresses that fact that conflicts are impossible to avoid; the challenge is to handle them effectively when they occur.

II.   In a *functional conflict,* participants achieve the best possible outcome, unlike a *dysfunctional conflict,* where the outcome falls short of what is possible.

        A.   Integration versus polarization describes how participants in a dysfunctional conflict regard each other as polar opposites, while participants in a functional conflict recognize that they are integrated or in a difficult situation together.

        B.   Cooperation versus opposition means that cooperation is possible in interpersonal conflicts, although participants in a dysfunctional conflict see each other as opponents.

        C.   Confirmation versus disconfirmation occurs in functional conflicts, where participants disagree but are not disagreeable.

        D.   Agreement versus coercion is described when, in destructive conflicts, participants use coercion to get what they want instead of finding ways to reach an agreement.

        E.   De-escalation versus escalation addresses the fact that in functional conflicts the participants solve more problems than they create, while in dysfunctional conflicts the problems grow larger instead of smaller.

        F.   Focusing versus drifting is the idea that, in dysfunctional conflicts, the participants drift away from the original problem and bring in other issues.

        G.   Foresight versus shortsightedness occurs when foresight is a feature of functional conflicts, while shortsightedness can produce dysfunctional conflicts.

        H.   Positive versus negative results describes the notion that functional conflicts have positive results, such as finding a solution that works, while a dysfunctional conflict has negative results, such as neither participant receiving what they want, and threatens the future of the relationship.

III.   Conflict styles are the default styles people have for handing conflict.

        A.   *Avoidance* occurs when people ignore or stay away from conflict either physically or conversationally.

        B.   *Accommodation* occurs when we allow others to have their own way rather than asserting our own point of view.

        C.   *Competition* is a win/lose approach to conflict that involves high concern for self and low concern for others and can result in aggression.

            1.   *Passive aggression* occurs when a communicator expresses dissatisfaction in a disguised manner.

            2.   *Direct aggression* occurs when a communicator attacks the source of displeasure.

        D.   *Compromise* gives both people at least some of what they want, though both sacrifice part of their goals.

        E.   *Collaboration* seeks to apply *win/win problem solving* to conflict and involves a high degree of concern for both self and others; the goal is to find a solution that satisfies the needs of everyone involved.

IV.   Conflict exists in relational systems as it is determined by the people who are involved; when two people are involved in a long-term relationship they develop their own *relational conflict style,* which is a pattern of managing disagreements that repeats itself over time.

    A.   *Complementary conflict style* is when partners use different but mutually reinforcing behaviors, while *symmetrical conflict style* is when both people use the same tactics, and *parallel conflict style* shifts between complementary and symmetrical patterns from one issue to another.

        1.   *Escalatory spiral* is when partners treat each other with matching hostility so that threats and insults lead to more threats and insults.

        2.   *De-escalatory spiral* results if the participants withdraw from one another instead of facing their problems.

    B.   There is an interaction between emotional closeness and aggression that is broken down as follows.

        1.   Nonintimate-aggressive communication occurs when partners dispute issues without dealing with one another on an emotional level.

        2.   Nonintimate-nonaggresive communication occurs when the partners avoid conflicts and one another instead of facing issues head-on.

        3.   Intimate-aggressive combines aggression and intimacy.

        4.   Intimate-nonaggressive is when there is a low amount of attacking or blaming.

    C.   *Conflict Rituals* are unacknowledged but are real repeating patterns of interlocking behavior.

    D.   Variables in conflict styles include gender and culture.

        1.   There are small but measurable differences in the way women and men handle conflict, but the individual style of each communicator is more important than gender.

        2.   The ways in which people resolve conflicts vary from one culture to another.

    E.   Conflict management in practice has guidelines to best approach win-win problem solving.

        1.   Define your needs by deciding what you want or need.

        2.   Share your needs with the other person when the time and place is suitable and you are at your best.

        3.   Listen to the other person's needs.

        4.   Generate possible solutions by brainstorming.

        5.   Evaluate the possible solutions and choose the best one once all possibilities have been exhausted.

        6.   Implement the solution.

        7.   Follow up the solution to review the effects of the solution.

Chapter 11: Summary

Conflict is an expressed struggle between at least two interdependent parties who perceive incompatible goals, scarce resources, and interference from the other party in achieving their goals. An expressed struggle does not have to be verbal, but all the people involved must know that some disagreement exists. A perceived incompatible goal is when it appears that one person's gain is another's loss. Perceived scarce resources are things like affection, money, space, time, or anything that people believe there is not enough of to go around. People in a conflict are dependent upon each other, yet most people do not realize their interdependence. Conflicts are inevitable, and the challenge is to handle them effectively since they cannot be avoided.

Dysfunctional conflict is when the outcome falls short of what is possible and has a damaging effect on the relationship. A functional conflict is one where the best possible outcome is achieved and relationships can even be strengthened. In a dysfunctional conflict, participants regard each other as polar opposites, while participants in a functional conflict realize that they are integrated since they are in a difficult situation together. Participants in a dysfunctional conflict see each other as opponents, while a more functional view recognizes that cooperative problem solving is desirable. In functional conflicts the participants may disagree but use supportive behaviors to tackle the conflict. In dysfunctional conflicts the participants rely heavily on coercion to get what they want, while participants in functional conflicts avoid power plays and try using agreement instead. In destructive conflicts, problems seem to escalate instead of diminish. In destructive conflicts, participants drift from the original problem and bring in non-related issues instead of focusing on one subject at a time. Shortsightedness can produce dysfunctional conflicts, while foresight is a feature of functional conflicts. Dysfunctional conflict typically has two consequences: first, that no one is likely to get what was originally sought, and second, that the future of the relationship may be threatened. Functional conflicts have positive results, including the reward of successfully facing a challenge and the fact that relationship growth occurs.

There are five different styles of handling conflict. Avoidance occurs when people non-assertively ignore or stay away from conflict and can be physical or conversational. It often produces lose-lose results. Accommodation occurs when we allow others to have their own way rather than asserting our own view and produces a lose-win scenario. Competition is the flip side of accommodation and involves a high concern for self and a low concern for others and as such is win-lose. Passive aggression occurs when a communicator expresses dissatisfaction in a disguised manner, while direct aggression is when a participants lashes out to attack the source of displeasure. A compromise gives both participants at least some of what they want, though both sacrifice some of what they want. Collaboration involves a high degree of concern for both self and others and can lead to a win-win outcome where each person can get what she or he wants. Win-win problem solving is concerned with a solution that satisfies the needs of everyone involved. There is no best way to solve a conflict, and each conflict must be treated differently based on the situation and the other person and goals.

Conflict is relational, and when people are in a long-term relationship, they develop their own relational conflict style, which is a pattern of managing disagreements that repeats itself over time. There are three styles of conflict management: complementary conflict style, where the partners use different but mutually reinforcing behaviors; symmetrical conflict style, which is when both people use the same tactics; and parallel conflict style, which shifts between complementary and symmetrical patterns from one issue to another. An escalatory spiral can occur when partners treat each other with matching hostility, while a de-escalatory spiral results when partners withdraw from each other instead of facing their problems.

Nonintimate-Aggressive interaction is when partners dispute issues but without dealing with one another on an emotional level. Nonintimate-nonaggressive interaction is when partners avoid conflicts and one another. Intimate-aggressive interaction is when aggression and intimacy are combined. Intimate-nonaggressive interaction is when partners confront one another but with a low amount of attacking or blaming.

Conflict rituals are unacknowledged but very real repeating patterns of interlocking behavior and can be a problem when they become the only way relational partners handle their conflicts. Two variables that affect the way people handle conflict are gender and culture.

Collaborative conflict management requires seven skills: define your needs, share your needs with the other person, listen to the other person's needs, generate possible solutions, evaluate the possible solutions and choose the best one, implement the solution, and follow up the solution.

Chapter 11: Key Terms

For each of these terms, define the term, give an example, and explain the significance of the term.

1. Accommodation

2. Avoidance

3. Collaboration

4. Competition

5. Complementary conflict style

6. Compromise

7. Conflict

8. Conflict ritual

9. De-escalatory spiral

10. Direct aggression

11. Dysfunctional conflict

12. Escalatory spiral

13. Functional conflict

14. Parallel conflict style

15. Passive aggression

16. Relational conflict style

17. Symmetrical conflict style

18. Win-win problem solving

Chapter 11: Review Questions

These questions are designed to help you better understand the concepts from this chapter and also allow you the opportunity to put the information into your own words. For practice true/false and multiple-choice questions, please refer to the course website.

1. Define conflict and provide an explanation of each of the defining features.

2. What are the two consequences of dysfunctional conflict?

3. What are the five different styles for handling conflict?

4. What are the three styles of conflict management?

5. What are the seven skills for collaborative conflict management?

Chapter 11: Thinking Outside the Box: Synthesizing Your Knowledge

These questions are designed to help connect the course material from previous chapters.

1. What is the relationship between functional and dysfunctional conflict as it relates to confirming and disconfirming communication climates (Chapter 10)?

2. What are some of the potential defining intercultural variables (Chapter 2) that may affect conflict styles?

Chapter 11: Answers to Review Questions

1. Define conflict and provide an explanation of each of the defining features.

   Conflict is an expressed struggle between at least two interdependent parties who perceive incompatible goals, scarce resources, and interference from the other party in achieving their goals. (1) Expressed struggle captures the notion that conflict does not exist unless all the people involved know that the disagreement exists even if the expressed struggle is not verbalized. (2) Perceived incompatible goals means that the goals of those involved are mutually exclusive, but that is not always the case as mutually satisfying answers can be agreed upon. (3) Perceived scarce resources occurs when people believe there are not enough resources, such as time, money, affection, and space to go around. (4) Interdependence captures the notion that people in a conflict are dependent upon each other. (5) Inevitability addresses that conflicts are impossible to avoid and the challenge is to handle them effectively when they occur.

2. What are the two consequences of dysfunctional conflict?

   First, rarely does anyone get what he or she originally sought. Second, the future of the relationship may be threatened.

3. What are the five different styles for handling conflict?

   (1) Avoidance occurs when people nonassertively ignore or stay away from conflict; it can be physical or conversational. (2) Accommodation occurs when we allow others to have their own way rather than asserting our own view; this produces a lose-win scenario. (3) Competition is the flip side of accommodation and involves a high concern for self and a low concern for others. (4) A compromise gives both participants at least some of what they want, though both sacrifice some of what they want. (5) Collaboration involves a high degree of concern for both self and others.

4. What are the three styles of conflict management?

   (1) The complementary conflict style is evidenced when the partners use different but mutually reinforcing behaviors. (2) Symmetrical conflict style is seen when both people use the same tactics. (3) Parallel conflict styles are those which shift between complementary and symmetrical patterns from one issue to another.

5. What are the seven skills for collaborative conflict management?

   The seven skills that are needed for collaborative conflict management are: define your needs, share your needs with the other person, listen to the other person's needs, generate possible solutions, evaluate the possible solutions and choose the best one, implement the solution, and follow up the solution.

Chapter 11: Answers to Thinking Outside the Box

1. What is the relationship between functional and dysfunctional conflict as it relates to confirming and disconfirming communication climates (Chapter 10)?

   Functional conflict is characterized by a confirming communication climate. Dysfunctional conflict exists in a disconfirming communication climate. In a functional conflict, participants achieve the best possible outcome, unlike in a dysfunctional conflict, where the outcome falls short of what is possible. Creating a positive climate can be achieved through the use of strategies that increase the odds of expression that leads to positive relational climates. Reducing defensiveness can be achieved by sending supportive rather than defense-provoking messages.

2. What are some of the potential defining intercultural variables (Chapter 2) that may affect conflict styles?

   Conflict styles vary by culture. The ways in which people resolve conflicts vary from one culture to another. Cultural values and norms are captured by five defining features that shape the way members of a culture communicate and express conflict. High- versus low-context: Low-context culture uses language primarily to express thoughts, feelings, and ideas as directly as possible, while high-context culture relies heavily on subtle, often nonverbal cues to maintain social harmony and is therefore less likely to directly express conflict. Individualism versus collectivism can be described as members of an individualistic culture viewing their primary responsibility as helping themselves, leading to open conflict expression, whereas members of collectivistic cultures feel loyalties and obligations to the in-group. Power distance describes the degree to which members of a society accept an unequal distribution of power, so in low-power-distance cultures, members are more likely to express conflict toward those with more power. Uncertainty avoidance is a term used to reflect the degree to which members of a culture feel threatened by ambiguous situations and how much they try to avoid them, and conflict expression varies accordingly. Achievement culture societies place a high value on material success, and conflict is then more likely to be expressed, while a nurturing culture regards the support of relationships as an especially important goal.

Chapter 12: Communication in Families and at Work

SQ3R in Action

Generate an SQ3R chart for this chapter here:
http://www.teach-nology.com/web_tools/graphic_org/sq3r

Survey

Skim the title, key terms, chapter outline, objectives ("You should understand" and "You should be able to"), headings, tables, photos, cartoons, figures, charts, and items in the margin. Glance at the titles of the Focus on Research, Reflection, Film Clips, Self-Assessment, and Dark Side. At the end of each chapter, look over the Summary, Critical Thinking Probes, Ethical Challenges, Skill Builder, and Resources.

Question

Ask yourself questions. What do you know about these topics from your own life experiences and from other classes? Ask these six questions in each section: who, what, when, where, how, and why?

Read

Take one heading at a time and read to find the answers to the questions you've posed.

Recite

In your own words, say the answer aloud and then write it out.

Review

Review each section and then review the whole chapter. This is a good time to use the activities at the end of each chapter and the activities and the sample exams on the course website. Remember to periodically review the previous chapters as well.

Chapter 12: Outline

(Italicized words are key terms.)

I.   There are different types of family communication, and a *family* is a *system* with two or more interdependent people who have a common history and a present reality and expect to influence each other in the future; within families, communication between each pair of members has its own characteristics.
  A.   Spouses/Partners communicate in a way that reflects their personal style and their understanding of what a relationship should be like.
  B.   Parent-child family communication becomes more complex with children.

1. Patterns of interaction change as members of a family can form different dyads which form coalitions that both enrich and complicate family communication.
2. Family members must manage the connection-autonomy dialectic, as it is normal for the needs of connection and autonomy to change as children grow up, with children needing more connection when they are young and more autonomy as they age.

C. Siblings have identifiable communication strategies for maintaining their relationships, including confirmation, humor, social support, and escape.

II. There are similar characteristics, or elements, of communication regardless of the type of family.

A. All families are communication systems whose members interact with one another to form a whole and possess a number of characteristics.
1. Family members are interdependent, since one family member's feelings and behaviors affect all the other members.
2. A family is more than the sum of its parts; to understand a family you must see it as a whole.
3. Families have systems within the larger system.
4. Family systems are affected by their environment, which includes personal and social forces.

B. The roles family members play which shape the way members communicate include kinship, functional, and social roles.

C. Family narratives unite a family and may reflect how members view each other or their values or reaffirm the family's identity.

D. Models for other relationships exist in families, as experiences in our *family of origin*, or the family in which we grew up, shape the way we communicate throughout life.

E. Communication rules exist in families, as families have their own set of rules that concern not only who may speak with or to whom but also how members may speak and topics of conversation.
1. *Conversation orientation* involves the degree to which families favor an open climate of discussion of a wide array of topics.
2. *Conformity orientation* refers to the degree to which family communication stresses uniformity of attitudes, values, and beliefs.

III. Effective communication in families is driven by some guidelines that can make any family's interaction more satisfying and rewarding.

A. Strive for closeness while respecting boundaries.
1. *Enmeshed families* suffer from too much consensus, too little independence, and a very high demand of loyalty.
2. *Disengaged families* occur when members of families have too little cohesion.
3. *Boundaries* are needed in order to set limits on family members' actions.

B. Strive for a moderate level of adaptability.
1. *Chaotic families* result when adaptability is too high, and it is one that has erratic leadership or no leadership at all.

2. *Rigid families* occur when adaptability is too low, when there is authoritarian leadership (usually in the hands of one parent), strict discipline, roles that are inflexible, and unchanging rules.

C. Confirming messages should be encouraged and are important to children and in marriages, as people need to feel valued.

D. Deal constructively with conflict.
1. Do not sweat the small stuff.
2. Focus on manageable issues.
3. Share appreciation as well as gripes.
4. Seek win-win solutions.

IV. Interpersonal communication occurs at work, and communication skills are important in every career.

A. Advancing your career involves interpersonal skills that can help you identify the type of work you will enjoy and excel at.

B. *Networking* is the process of deliberately meeting people and maintaining contacts to get career information, advice, and leads.

C. Interviewing for employment is a type of conversation that greatly differs from other conversations in terms of importance and structure.

V. Communicating in organizations is key, as new communication skills are needed once one joins an organization.

A. *Formal* and *informal communiction* occurs in most work settings, as people are identified by their roles and these roles combine to create formal communication, which is interaction that follows officially established channels.
1. *Upward communication* is when subordinates communicate with their bosses.
2. *Downward communication* is when managers address subordinates.
3. *Horizontal communication* occurs between people who don't have direct supervisor-subordinate relationships.
4. *Informal communication* is based on friendships, shared personal or career interests, and proximity.

B. Face-to-face and mediated relationships occur at work, as workers can communicate face to face or through electronic media, and many businesses have *virtual teams*, whose memberships transcend boundaries of location and time.

VI. Relationships in work groups matter, as good personal relationships are essential in a well-functioning team.

A. Personal skills in work groups are needed, as various relational roles such as encouraging participation, harmonizing, relieving tension, evaluating the group's emotional climate, giving praise, and listening thoughtfully need to be filled at one time or another in the life span of every group.

B. Group cultures develop, as working groups have their own organizational cultures which are stable, shared rules about how to behave and a set of values about what is important; these cultures include characteristics of communication like sociability, distribution of power, tolerance for new ideas, ways of managing conflict, and emotional support.

C.   Leadership, power, and influence in working groups emerge, as influence in groups comes not just from the *designated leader* or person with an official title but also from resources of *power* that can affect what happens in a group, such as expert power, reward power, coercive power, or referent power.

Chapter 12: Summary

A family is broadly defined to include many types of relationships, but essentially a family is a system with two or more interdependent people who have a common history and a present reality, and who expect to influence each other in the future. Within families communication differs among the different members, and the communication has its own characteristics.

Communication patterns of spouses/partners reflect their personal style and their understanding of what a relationship should be like. There are three basic couple types: independents, separates, and traditionals. Independent couples avoid traditional sex roles, while separate couples place a higher value on their individual freedom than on their relationship; traditional couples adhere to traditional sex roles. Independent couples do not avoid conflict. Separate and traditional couples tend to avoid conflict more than independent couples.

Gender roles offer another way to look at communication between partners. Stereotypically masculine communication emphasizes instrumental, task-related topics and is low in expressive, emotional content. Stereotypically feminine communication is high in expressiveness and low in instrumentality, while androgynous communication is high in both emotional and instrumentality. Undifferentiated communication is low in both instrumentality and expressiveness.

Family communication becomes more complex when children are present, since there are members of the family to form different dyads that can then form coalitions which can enrich and complicate family communication. Families must also try to manage the connection-autonomy dialectic, which changes as children age and become more independent. Siblings have identifiable communication strategies; these include such behaviors as confirmation, humor, social support, and escape. Sibling-to-sibling communication can be broken down into affection, hostility, and rivalry.

Families are systems, and they possess a number of characteristics that determine the way members communicate. Family members are interdependent; each event in a family is a reaction to the family's history, and each event shapes future interaction. A family is more than a sum of its parts and must been seen as a whole. Families have systems within the larger system. Family systems are affected by their environment, which includes personal and social forces. The roles that family members play shape the way members communicate. There are functional roles and social roles that dictates who does what within a family. Family narratives serve a variety of functions, including reaffirming the identity of the family and reflecting either a family's view of how members relate to one another or shared values.

Family interaction within the family of origin, which is the family in which we grow up, shapes our notion of how to communicate, but not all families communicate the same way. There are rules governing communication that are unspoken but understood and include who may speak with or to whom, how one may speak, and topics of conversation.

Conversation orientation is the degree to which families favor an open climate of discussion of a wide array of topics, while conformity orientation refers to the degree to which family communication stresses uniformity of attitudes, values, and beliefs. Families high in both conversation orientation and conformity orientation are consensual. Families high in conversation orientation and low in conformity orientation are pluralistic. And families that are both low in conversation orientation and high in conformity orientation are protective. Families low in both conversation orientation and conformity orientation are laissez-faire.

There are some general guidelines to follow to improve communication between family members and within a family. Strive for closeness while respecting boundaries. When cohesion is too high, a family may be enmeshed, which is to suffer from too much consensus, too little independence, and a very high demand for loyalty. If a family has too little cohesion they may be disengaged, or disconnected, with limited attachment to each other. The way to cope with these tensions is to create boundaries which are limits that are set on members' actions. Also, a family should strive for a moderate level of adaptability. Too much adaptability and a chaotic family results, which is one that has erratic or no leadership at all. A rigid family, or one with strict discipline and inflexible and unchanging roles, results from having a low adaptability level. A family should encourage confirming messages which communicate how we value another person. A family should also deal constructively with conflict by not sweating the small stuff, focusing on manageable issues, sharing appreciations as well as gripes, and seeking win-win solutions.

Interpersonal communication at work is just as important as it is in families or other personal relationships, and there are some steps to take to have a successful career. First is to advance your career by using interpersonal communication in determining and securing employment. In order to secure a job, networking, or the process of deliberately meeting people and maintaining contacts to get career information, advice, and leads, is advisable. The interview process is a chance to explore the fit between yourself and a prospective employer and is a conversation unlike other conversations. Interviews are much more purposeful, have structure, control, and a balance of participation that differs from other conversations. In order to do well in the interview, there are some guidelines to follow. Clarify the interviewer's goals, make a good first impression, get off to a good start, give clear, detailed answers, keep your answers focused, follow the interviewer's lead, and come prepared to answer the interviewer's questions.

New communication skills are needed inside a work organization. There is formal communication, which is interaction that follows officially established channels and is divided into three types. Upward communication is when subordinates communicate with their bosses; downward communication is when managers address the subordinates; and horizontal communication occurs between people who do not have direct supervisor-subordinate relationships. Informal communication is based on friendships, shared personal or career interests, and proximity.

People in working relationships can communicate either face-to-face or through mediated communication channels such as faxes, e-mail, telephone, and instant messaging. Some organizations have virtual teams whose membership transcends the boundaries of location and time.

Working in teams requires specific skills to be successful, and relational roles must be filled during the group's life. There are stages to a group's life. First is the orientation stage, when a team first starts working together and politeness and harmony are the norm; but, as time goes on, the group enters a state of conflict. Once the conflict has been settled, a team enters into an emergence stage, where members accept the team's decision. A fourth stage is reinforcement, where the team members not only accept the decision but endorse it.

Working groups have their own organizational culture, which is a set of shared rules about how to behave and what is important. Working group culture involves such things as sociability, distribution of power, tolerance for new ideas, ways of managing conflict, and emotional support. The designated leader is the person with an official title in a group, whereas other people can influence the group, such as any person with the resource of power that can affect what happens in a group next. Expert power is when individual members have an area of expertise or talent that can help the group. Reward power is when members reward one another. Coercive power is when members threaten or punish one another to get results. Referent power is the influence that comes when members like and respect each other.

Chapter 12: Key Terms

For each of these terms, define the term, give an example, and explain the significance of the term.

1. Boundaries

2. Chaotic family

3. Conformity orientation

4. Conversation orientation

5. Designated leader

6. Disengaged family

7. Downward communication

8. Enmeshed family

9. Family

10. Family of origin

11. Formal communication

12. Horizontal communication

13. Informal communication

14. Networking

15. Power

16. Rigid family

17. System

18. Upward communication

19. Virtual teams

Chapter 12: Review Questions

These questions are designed to help you better understand the concepts from this chapter and also allow you the opportunity to put the information into your own words. For practice true/false and multiple-choice questions, please refer to the course website.

1. Describe the four characteristics of family communication systems.

2. Define conversation orientation and conformity orientation, and identify the four possible configurations of families that result from high and low levels of each.

3. Effective communication in families is driven by moderate levels of adaptability. What types of families emerge when adaptability is too high, and when adaptability is too low?

4. What are the four tips for dealing constructively with conflict?

5. Identify and explain the four different types of power that individuals may possess.

Chapter 12: Thinking Outside the Box: Synthesizing Your Knowledge

These questions are designed to help connect the course material from previous chapters.

1. Which relational dialectic (Chapter 9) is especially relevant to families with children?

2. Explain how gender roles explain communication that occurs between relational partners and how this relates to the three approaches that represent the gender and language debate (Chapter 5).

Chapter 12: Answers to Review Questions

1. Describe the four characteristics of family communication systems.

   (1) Family members are interdependent, since one family member's feelings and behaviors affect all the other members. (2) A family is more than the sum of its parts, and to understand a family you must see it as a whole. (3) Families have systems within the larger system. (4) Family systems are affected by their environment, which includes personal and social forces.

2. Define conversation orientation and conformity orientation, and identify the four possible configurations of families that result from high and low levels of each.

   Conversation orientation is the degree to which families favor an open climate of discussion of a wide array of topics while conformity orientation refers to the degree to which family communication stresses uniformity of attitudes, values and beliefs. Families high in both conversation orientation and conformity orientation are consensual. Families high in conversation orientation and low in conformity orientation are pluralistic. Families low in both conversation orientation and high in conformity orientation are protective. Families low in both conversation orientation and conformity orientation are laissez-faire.

3. Effective communication in families is driven by moderate levels of adaptability. What types of families emerge when adaptability is too high, and when adaptability is too low?

   Chaotic families result when adaptability is too high, and it is one that has erratic leadership or no leadership at all. Rigid families occur when adaptability is too low, when there is authoritarian leadership (usually in the hands of one parent), strict discipline, roles that are inflexible, and unchanging rules.

4. What are the four tips for dealing constructively with conflict?

(1) Don't sweat the small stuff. (2) Focus on manageable issues. (3) Share appreciations as well as gripes. (4) Seek win-win solutions.

5. Identify and explain the four different types of power that individuals may possess.

Expert power is when individual members have an area of expertise or talent that can help the group. Reward power is when members reward one another. Coercive power is when members threaten or punish one another to get results. Referent power is the influence that comes when members like and respect each other.

Chapter 12: Answers to Thinking Outside the Box

1. Which relational dialectic (Chapter 9) is especially relevant to families with children?

The dialectical perspectives on relational dynamics is another way of explaining interaction in relationships and is focused on dialectical tensions or conflicts that arise when two opposing or incompatible forces exist simultaneously. The connection-autonomy dialectic is where we want to be close to others but also seek to be autonomous; this is an internal struggle. Family members must manage the connection-autonomy dialectic, as it is normal for the needs of connection and autonomy to change as children grow up, with children needing more connection when they are young and more autonomy as they age.

2. Explain how gender roles explain communication that occurs between relational partners and how this relates to the three approaches that represent the gender and language debate (Chapter 5).

Gender roles offer another way to look at communication between partners. Stereotypically masculine communication emphasizes instrumental, task-related topics and is low in expressive, emotional content. Stereotypically feminine communication is high in expressiveness and low in instrumentality, while androgynous communication is high in both emotional and instrumentality. Undifferentiated communication is low in both instrumentality and expressiveness. There are three approaches that represent three different sides in the gender and language debate. The first approach, called fundamental differences, argues that men and women are fundamentally different and can be described as being members of distinct cultures. The second approach is important differences, which describes a theory in which scholars acknowledge that there are some significant differences in the way men and women use language. The third approach is the minor differences approach, which states that the link between sex and language use is not clear-cut.